Imperial
Chinese
Art

帝
國

Imperial Chinese Art

中
國
藝
術

Lin Yutang

GREENWICH HOUSE
Distributed by Crown Publishers, Inc.
New York

This 1983 edition is published by Greenwich House,
a division of Arlington House, Inc.,
distributed by Crown Publishers, Inc.

Printed in Hong Kong by South China Printing Co.

Library of Congress Catalog Card no: 83-81549

ISBN 0-517-416476

h g f e d c b a

TABLE OF CONTENTS

Notes on Spelling of Chinese Names

Chinese concepts corresponding to English words are spelled as single words, and not as separate syllables. Thus I write *Hatamen Gate* as the Chinese visualise it, and not as *Ha Ta Men*, as many sinologists do. Similarly, I refer to the *Wanshoushan* on the *Kunminghu* Lake of *Yihoyuan*, instead of *Wan Shou Shan* on *Kun Ming Hu* of *I Ho Yuan*. The latter gives an effect rather like writing *Pic Ca Dil Ly Cir Cus*.

As is commonly done in newspapers, I have eliminated the aspirate marks. The Wade system was never meant for a running text, but for beginners' notes on pronunciation only. My name, for instance, with aspirate and tone marks included, would have to be written as Lin[2] Yü[3] T'ang[2].

For the sake of simplicity, I have also substituted *sh* and *y* for the more usual spellings *hs* and *ih*. In fact, *hs* is pronounced as *sh* (which covers a lot of sounds, phonetically speaking); *hsi* is not very different from the English *she*. The *ih* in *chih*, *shih* and the *û* in *tsû*, *ssû* (also *tzû*, *szû*) are very difficult to pronounce correctly anyway and most English people make an ordinary *i* serve as an approximation. I have written them as *chy*, *shy*, *tsy*, *sy*—as in the Empress Dowager's name *Tsyshi*, instead of the spelling of *Tzûhsi*.

L. Y.

N. B. — In his *Essay on the Art of Peking*, Mr. Peter Swann uses the more conventional spellings, not those explained above by Dr. Lin.

LIST OF ILLUSTRATIONS

8

LIST OF MAPS AND DIAGRAMS

The illustrations in the text
are from contemporary wood engravings.

THE SPIRIT OF OLD PEKING

BEFORE 1949 when the Communist régime took over the whole of China and effectively closed the country to visitors, Peking was one of the world's great capitals and attracted people from all over the world. Many have claimed that Paris and Peking are the two most beautiful cities in the world; and some who know both place Peking first. Almost all who have visited Peking have come to love it, for like other capitals such as London, Paris, Rome and Vienna, it inspires affection. And like all great cities, Peking grows on one, its elusive charm being as inescapable as it is difficult to analyse and describe. Great old cities are like tolerant grandmothers. They represent to their children a world vaster than one can explore or exhaust, and one is happy merely to grow up under their all-embracing protection. Each year one learns something new about a city like Peking. Only a brave man, after living ten years in Paris or Rome, would claim to know the city. This is equally true of Peking, a city to explore, a city not merely to visit for three days or even three weeks, but above all a city to live in. In the early days of the Chinese Republic, I knew many Europeans who came to visit Peking for a week or month but decided to settle there for life. Once you have lived in Peking, it lives on with you after you have left it.

Every city should have its own character. A lady can have charm without character, but a city cannot. All old cities are the outcome of centuries of growth; they bear the scars of wars and the marks of historical events, they stand witness to the dreams and ambitions of men of the past. Just as Napoleon and Haussmann left their marks on Paris, and Empress Maria-Teresa and Franz-Joseph on Vienna, so the Emperors Yunglo and Chienlung have left their marks on Peking—especially Chienlung, who restored, retouched and beautified every historical monument in his sixty-year reign of peace and prosperity to make it the magnificent city that it was.

Yet a city can never be the creation of a single man. Generations of men by their way of life and their achievements give it their heritage and stamp their character upon it. Dynasties come and go, and tyrants rise and fall, but in Peking the life of the common people continues unperturbed. In the sixteenth century the eunuchs spread terror among the scholar officials, and one eunuch in particular, Wei Tsungshien, had his portrait hung in every city throughout the nation, to which the people were compelled to bow. Wei left his mark in Peking, at Piyunsy in the Western Hills, which he helped to beautify. But like the rest, he too passed by. With eternal cities, such short moments pass and

11

are forgotten. The happy life of the people goes on. Every city is greater than the personalities which momentarily dominate it.

Three important elements have combined to give Peking its unique character: nature, art, and the life and character of the people. Nature provides the physical environment; the art of man has adorned it with towers, palaces and temples; the way of life of the common people, rich and poor, their habits, customs and festivals, determine whether the life of the city is to be easy, leisurely and creative, or harsh with the hustle and bustle of money-mad pettifogging merchants. Peking is fortunate in that all three elements combine in harmony. The charm of Peking lies as much in the opulence of the imperial palaces as in the quiet, sometimes unbelievably rural aspect of the households. It is thus a city where one can both be stimulated by art, architecture and colourful festivals and at the same time enjoy the quiet and peace of a country life.

In this book we shall examine these three elements in turn. The very richness of Peking architecture determines that a large proportion must be given to it—to the palaces, temples and imperial tombs. But it is not the Eiffel Tower that makes Paris what it is, but the café life in Montmartre and the Boulevard St. Germain that gives it its special flavour. This is also true of Peking. The palaces may impress the tourist, but the real charm of Peking resides in its common people, in the life of the streets. One can never find out exactly what makes the poor in Peking so gay and courageous; it is part of them, of their philosophy of living.

The first impression of Peking is its climate—an incredibly blue sky, and sunny, dry cold in winter, in summer a plentiful cool rain. Then comes the opulence and splendour of its buildings, and finally the humour, patience and politeness of a people governed by centuries of custom. The sky is clear and open, the palaces stretch out in vast distances with turrets and wing towers, and the rickshaw boys endlessly crack jokes and laugh at others' mishaps. Generosity is the keynote: generosity in the elements, in the scale of architecture and in the temperament and spirit of man. Life is essentially simple, requirements few and easy to get—or so it was until some ten years ago. This simplicity springs from the natural gaiety and rugged strength of the north, a gaiety coming from a basic realistic recognition that life is good but short, to be endured and enjoyed as best one can. The harsh jangle of modern business life was unknown. In this simplicity of living and thinking, man's spirit was liberated and great art was produced.

The physical characteristics of a city are determined very largely by its location and climate, by the sunshine which colours it, the sky which reflects it and the air through which we see it. The Peking weather always seems to make up its mind decisively, usually in favour of sunshine; dry in winter, wet in summer. Thunderstorms come in July and August and regularly cease with the onset of October, only to return quite late in spring. There are no half measures. When it rains, it rains hard, and when it clears, it does so completely. The well known drizzles of April in the south are unknown here. ("*On the Chingming festival the drizzle lingers on, and the wayfarer's heart is sad and full,*" says a famous poem.) The dryness of the climate ensures that the ground dries quickly after a night's rainfall, and the trees smile again in their resplendent green, brighter in the clear air. The white pagoda on Jade Fountain Hill appears so clearly through the clean air that it seems much nearer than it is.

It is true that in Peking one revels in the blue of the sky but eats the dust of the earth. "On a windless day there are three inches of dust, and on a rainy day there is mud all over the ground," says a proverb. But this is very largely a matter of pavements. On the broad Hatamen Boulevard mule-cart roads, some

fifteen feet wide, line both sides of the central pavement. Asphalt roads cannot hold the dust, which is clearly demonstrated on windy days when one rides through the well-paved Legation Quarters. On the other hand, studies made by the Rockefeller Medical Institute in Peking have proved that on account of the strong sunshine, the dust has an unusually low percentage of bacteria. The sun beats the dust into a pale buff or grey. The walls of the houses are uniformly grey or buff, set off here and there by the terra-cotta pink walls of an old temple, while the lichen-coated roofs are black or a slate-grey. Such clean, solid colours are seen to advantage only in a clear sunny climate.

Much as one may love a city, before it can be called ideal, it should be possible to escape easily to the hills and streams. Even if one does not go out to them very often, the knowledge that they are accessible makes city living endurable. Peking is fortunately situated, within ten to fifteen miles of the Western Hills, which lead gradually into deeper and higher mountains. Here are found ancient temples, several centuries old, and a clear stream from a vigorous spring, whose water feeds the Sea Palaces within the city. The Shiangshan Hunting Park is a huge area of parkland, graced with pagodas, old trees and rockeries. It is known

13

A	Tehshengmen	a	Zoo
B	Antingmen	b	Five Pagoda Temple
C	Tungchymen	c	Great Bell Temple
D	Chihuamen	d	Yellow Temple
E	Tungpienmen	e	Yunghokung (Lama Temple)
F	Hatamen	f	Coal Hill
G	Chienmen	g	Shyshahai
H	Shunchymen (Shüanwu-men)	h	Altar of Earth
I	Shipienmen	i	Altar of Sun
J	Pingtsemen	j	Altar of Moon
K	Shichymen	k	White Pagoda Temple
L	Changyimen	m	Roman Catholic Church (Peitang)
M	Nanshimen (Yu-anmen)	n	Mohammedan Mosque
N	Yungtingmen	p	Tachingmen (changed to Chunghuamen in 1912)
O	Chiangtsemen	q	Site of the old Examination Hall
P	Shawomen	r	Observatory
1	Inner City	s	Goldfish Ponds
2	Imperial City	t	Temple of Agriculture
3	Forbidden City	u	Temple of Heaven
4	Outer City	v	Tienningsy
555	Wall		

as Emperor Chienlung's Deer Park, and contained many rich men's villas. This area and the Patachu ("Eight Great Places") can now be easily reached by car within half an hour from Shichymen. The white marble pagoda of the Jade Fountain Hill glistens in the sun, and of course the Longevity Hill (Wanshoushan) of the Summer Palace is always visible in the distance. The small local streams of Peking all come from the great mountains in the west and, while some are muddy and sluggish, the Jade Fountain spring is unbelievably clear and so cool that no one has dared to bathe in it. The blue sky lends it the colour of clear emerald green from which it gets its name.

Standing at the Sleeping Buddha Temple in the Western Hills or on the top of the Piyunsy stupa, one has a bird's-eye view of the imperial city. The five-mile long massive grey walls are visible, and on clear days even the distant gate-towers appear as blotches of grey. Surprisingly large areas of green stand out above the glistening yellow palace roofs. These are the distant Sea Palaces.

Since Peking has been the capital of China for centuries, it has a population which is both northern and southern. But the majority are northerners, taller in stature, vigorous and strong. There is no suggestion of the indolence of the south, of the white-faced Soochow boys and the tender-waisted Shanghai ladies. The predominant colours seem to be dust and blue, but the ubiquitously blue-clad

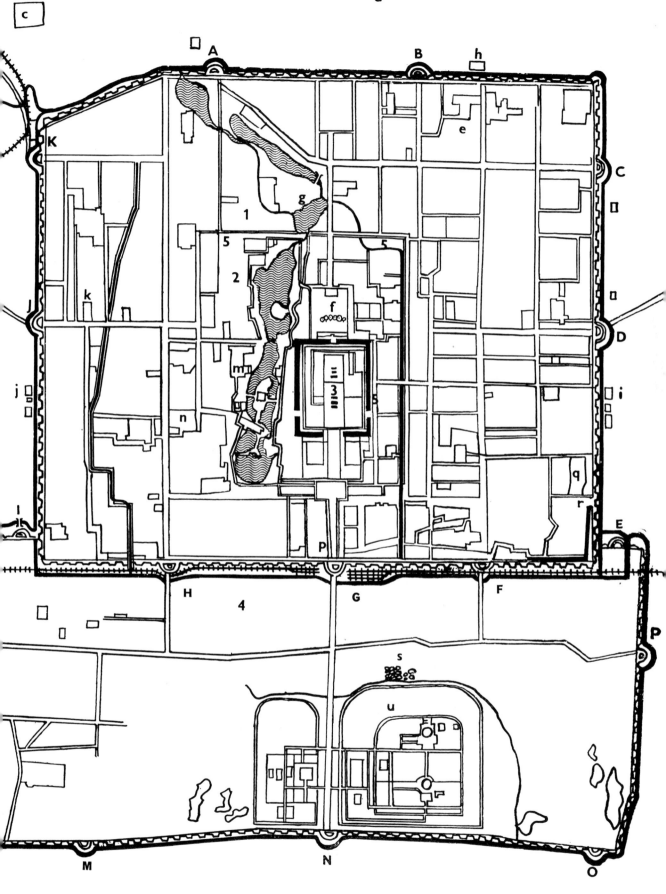

population contrasts here and there with Mongolians and Tibetans, dressed in long sacks, their heads often clean-shaven, their tall figures a little grotesque on the puny donkeys or Mongolian ponies they ride. The deep maroon or yellow robes of Lama priests also provide touches of striking contrast, the colours differentiating two main sects. During festivals and in spring, the women, especially in the country districts, come out in bright solid colours of red, lavender and green.

The life of the people in Peking occupies a separate chapter, but here we must briefly mention the quality of these northern people as one of the features of Peking life. They are basically conservative, with all the good and bad which conservatism implies. They do not take kindly to modern innovations, and they do not care. They prefer their etiquette and their rules of behaviour, formed by centuries of custom and religious beliefs, their mile-long funeral processions, their ancient lullabies, and the private date and pomegranate trees in their yards. Modern, educated Chinese tend to feel that their favourite ideas and complacent values receive a rude jolt when confronted with the verities of Old Peking. Foreign residents look on, fascinated by the art and teased by the humorous proverbs and folkways of the Chinese. Some reserve their judgment and wish only that the northern and eastern rooms were not separated by an open yard, that the electric lights were a little brighter and the telephone service a little better. Some become scholars, learn written Chinese and delve into the history and literature of the past; these persons are usually regarded as "queer" by their compatriots, tending to shake public confidence in "white prestige." Their wives swear that they will not leave Peking and cannot do without the wonderful amahs, who look after their babies as if they were their own.

What really matters for tourists and residents alike in any city is the people with whom one has contact, the house servants, the waiters at restaurants, the rickshaw boys or taxi-drivers. They can annoy for little or no reason, or by their order, smoothness and politeness, they can make life a gratuitous pleasure. Peking rickshaw boys always babble as they run, and if one knew the language one might enter into long, cheerful conversations all the way, in which the rickshaw boy would be more likely to give than receive advice. A Peking amah is sweet, quiet, and gifted with a high sense of self-respect. The Peking waiter is an institution, a man who has discovered the secret of showing extreme courtesy without the loss of personal dignity. A Tungshinglou waiter, in a blue gown and with a white towel across his shoulder, stands up and almost shouts his cordial greeting as if you were a person of the greatest importance. While he does his best to attend to your comforts, he looks at you straight in the eyes and talks in his broad generous voice. In his heart he knows that you too are trying to make a living the same as he, while he has a pride in his profession. These are the people who are the strength of the population of an old, cultured city, and whose instinctive sense of conduct and courtesy oils the wheels of everyday living. There are of course crooked politicians and *nouveaux riches* who love to swagger and impress, but if they stay long enough, even they mellow and become absorbed into the simplicity and dignity of the old way of life. Peking is the old woman who teaches them how to live—with comfort and ease.

What is the spirit of old Peking? Is it in its great, glistening palaces and old temples? Is it in the pleasances and huge park areas? Is it in some long-bearded peanut-vendor, standing over his stall with the natural dignity of his venerable age? One does not know. One cannot put it into words. It is there, with the ineffable charm of centuries. Then one day perhaps comes the shattering realization that it is a way of life, belonging to other worlds, other times, mature, pagan and cheerful and strong, bespeaking a re-evaluation of all values—a unique creation of the spirit of man.

1. The Tower of the
Thousand Buddhas,
Winter Palace.

16

THE SEASONS

THE CLIMATE of a city plays a large part in the life of its people. The Greek view of life, and one is tempted to say even the clarity of its prose, is a reflection of the open Aegean Sea and the Mediterranean sun; the cult of the nude would hardly be imaginable in Norway. In India, the forest sages learned great wisdom because the climate was so hot that the only thing to do was to sit in the shade and meditate. The French open-air café is made possible by the warm climate of France. Such an institution would be impossible in a climate with violent cold and frequent rains. The English heavy breakfast and high tea grew out of the need to "fortify" oneself before braving the cold in the morning, and the desirability of a good fire and hot tea when escaping from the afternoon fogs. I am inclined to believe that the cold and the muffler have even had an influence in producing an accent like that of the English, in which one tightens the guttural muscles and hardly opens the mouth. The Peking dialect also has broad, clean-cut vowels, which are pleasant to the ear. These leisurely measured rhythms are possible only when the speaker is not gripped by cold.

Peking is situated on the 40th latitude. Climatically speaking, this means little, since so are New York, the southern tip of Italy and northern Greece and Iran. But Peking's climate is sunny in winter, with a plentiful rainfall in summer—a combination which seems ideal. The god of thunder always leaves Peking in October for the entire winter. A thin coating of ice forms on lakes and ponds and village children skate by just sliding in their cloth shoes, sometimes aided by hay tied round them. (According to Ser Marco Polo, Kublai Khan and the Mongol princes had skating parties.) The dry cold is invigorating. The tips of the Western Hills may have a covering of snow, but this is rare. The dry, thin, bright sun beats the dust into a clear, whitish buff, and in the country the soil cracks with the frost and cold.

In winter the lambs on the Western Hills grow heavy wool, and the people retreat behind closed doors with heavy, padded cloth screens. These are strengthened with wooden boards across the middle which prevent the wind from rattling them. Inside the wine-shops, steam rises in the air mingled with men's breath. The smell of *paikan*, which is 70 per cent alcohol, blends with the aroma of onion and fried mutton. Men and women sensibly wear fur on the inside of their gowns; and lamb or sheepskin is so cheap that even rickshaw pullers can afford them. The tails of their gowns grow coated with a whole winter's dust. The older generation wear a form of *toufeng*, a headdress made of cloth or silk,

2. The stupa at the
Blue Cloud Temple, Piyunsy.

19

usually black or red, tied over their heads and around their necks and shoulders. One of the most sensible customs is to have the trouser ends tied up with braid, which keeps the dust out and the legs warm. Alternatively, a padded trouser-sheath is worn over the under-trousers. This is tied round the ankles, but the top of the back is cut away and is fastened in front, to prevent a too-bulky appearance at the back. Thus, it keeps the legs warm but does not interfere with the free movement of the legs.

The houses are heated by means of charcoal braziers. The glowing charcoal is prepared in the kitchen until it is smokeless and then placed in copper basins and covered with hot ashes. The windows are covered with a heavy, durable but flexible paper called *maochy*, which can be rolled up. The paper acts as an insulator against heat and cold. However, the real protection against the cold is provided by the *kang*. This is a large, wide couch built into the room, usually extending along its entire length. It is seven or eight feet deep, the depth being equal to the length of an average bed. This *kang*, made of mud and bricks, is both stoked and ventilated from the outside of the house. It serves as a seat in daytime and as a bed at night. In poor families, where heating is necessarily limited, in winter a whole family may sleep on one heated *kang*. Reed mats cover the floor, or rich, heavy carpets in the homes of the wealthy. As people wear pyjamas, of varying thicknesses and number of layers, under their gowns, they do not change into night attire—a convenience when the weather is cold. Under-wear is changed, but not for sleeping. Some extremely poor Manchus sleep naked, to save wear and tear on their pyjamas!

There may be a whistling wind outside, or dry twigs may break off and fall upon the roof, but the room is cosy and warm. Peace descends upon the house at night. It is both silent and yet not silent. The music of the hutungs begins slowly. (A hutung roughly corresponds to the English word "alley".) In ancient times, the bells from the Bell Tower kept the watch of the night, but this was replaced by night-watchmen, employed by the city, who walk the streets striking the watch on a wooden knocker, three knocks for midnight and five knocks for dawn. The music of the hutungs comes from the vendors' cries, soft, low and distant, and long drawn out. I have heard some Europeans comment on this music of the *hutungs* as a most troublesome disturbance of sleep, while others call it unique, soothing, and indispensable to slumber.

In summer and winter, the vendors' cries fill the *hutungs*. They alone obtrude upon the quiet of an otherwise silent neighbourhood and give it a gentle stir of life. The vendors are invaluable to the housewife who, thanks to their services, does not have to go to the market if she does not want to. The traders bring their wares to the house. The fish man may come at about ten in the morning, or the seller of ladies' notions, needle and thread, ribbons and children's toys, may come at any hour of the day. Another makes a business of touring the alleys to collect bottles in exchange for matches. His visit is unpredictable, but when he does come the thrifty housewife has her empty bottles ready and gets a free supply of matches. These visits are not really so frequent as to disturb the peace of the alley, but they do bring life to the *hutung* area.

The various street traders are recognised by their different signals. On a lazy, hot afternoon, the twanging of a large tuning fork means that the children may have their hair cut. The barber is invited into the yard, and if she likes, the mother may provide her own basin and towels. The sound of clanging copper saucers announces the seller of *suanmeitang*, a cold drink made of sweet and sour crab apples.

Nothing is more pleasant than to hear at night, towards eleven, the clanging of porcelain spoon against bowl, the signal of the *yuanshiao* peddler, who sells

3. Front view of the Temple of Heaven, showing the marble balustrades.

little dumplings served in hot syrup. Day or night comes the cry of a vendor of luscious persimmons, frozen in the cold weather, or, for the children, *ping-tang hulu*, small sugar-coated plums, five or six on a stick, coloured red for effect. One reads in short stories of the Sung period, as far back as the twelfth century, of a seller of roasted pheasant or partridge going about in the residential sections. Dumplings, or hot noodles, cold roasts for night snacks—a housewife can buy many little luxuries without even leaving the house. The itinerant portable restaurant is not a bad idea, especially when one does not have a telephone.

One peculiarity of these tradesmen is the way they cup their palms behind their ears. One would imagine that their long and always rhythmic calls would carry farther by cupping their mouth, but they seem to believe that the sounds are carried better when they cup their ears—presumably because they hear it better themselves then.

Then spring comes. On Shichymen Boulevard or Hatamen Boulevard people in rickshaws and carriages come back from the suburbs with sprigs of peach blossom, the signals of spring's arrival. Within the city are endless temples and parks. Visits are arranged to see the lilacs at an old temple outside Chienmen or the peonies at Tsungshiaosy, or even farther out towards the Temple of Agriculture, inside the south gate of the Outer City, to see the budding mulberry leaves. One may go to the Tungyomiao just outside Chihuamen Gate to worship the various popular gods of matrimony or of longevity. Tienchiao (Bridge of Heaven) outside Chienmen, an area of popular amusements, comes to life with its boxers, acrobats and open-air theatres, and flower shows are staged at Changtien. Temple fairs are held all the year round, especially at Lungfosy Temple in the East City and Hukuosy Temple in the West City. They go the round of the month by rotation, on fixed days, such as the first, eleventh and twenty-first at one, and the third, thirteenth and twenty-third at another.

Outside the city, at Paomachang near Poyunkuan, lies the race course. Farther on, at Wanshousy, one can take a boat on the river, which leads straight to the Summer Palace. A day may well be spent at the Western Hills, in visits to the Jade Fountain Hill or the Sleeping Buddha Temple (Wofosy), or a little farther away to the Patachu ("Eight Great Places"). People who can afford spring holidays go out to the country to see the Ming Tombs or the Great Wall at Chuyungkuan.

Because of its northern latitude, spring in Peking is short and autumn merges easily into winter. Before one knows it, spring slips into summer, the ideal season in this cold country. In the many park areas are tea shops, where one can sip tea under the old cypresses, lolling on a low rattan chair and watching the world pass by. On Sundays, the Central Park is crowded, but on weekdays the Park and the Temple of Agriculture are peaceful, shady and quiet. To sit in an open-air tea garden, close by the historic walls and imperial gates, spending twenty cents for a bowl of noodles, served by ever-courteous waiters who know the art of pleasing, seems to express the essence of Peking life. Like a visit to a temple bazaar, it seems to breathe an atmosphere of ease and well-being. Ease, a knowledge of the past, and an appreciation of history, create a sense of the evanescence of time and the detached view of life which are the essence of Chinese literature and art at their best. This is not reality in the raw, but life recreated and reflected in the mind of man, which invests it with a dreamlike quality.

In autumn, the wild geese which have fattened all summer long in the great marshy areas south of the city, and the herons which have hidden in the thickets along the streams, start on their annual migration southwards. The parks and the Western Hills are ablaze with reds and purples. The rich red soil of the hills combines with the reflection of the blue sky to create the famous purple slopes

4. View of the Summer Palace, showing typical multiple roofing.

23

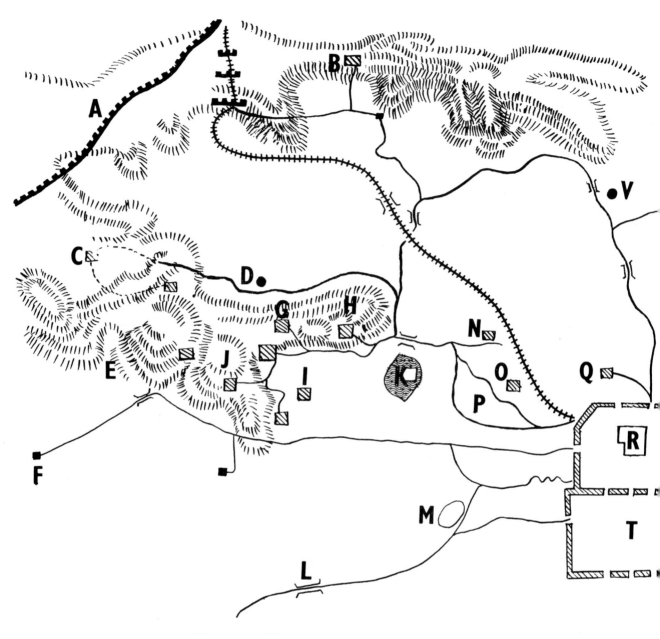

Peking and Environs today

A	Great Wall	L	Marco Polo Bridge
B	Ming Tombs	M	Race Course
C	Miaofeng Shan (Pilgrimage)	N	Old Summer Palace (Yuanmingyuan)
D	Hot Springs	O	Big Bell Temple
E	Imperial Mummy	P	Zoo
F	Mentoukow (Coal pits)	Q	Yellow Temple
G	Sleeping Buddha	R	Forbidden City
H	Jade Fountain Hill	S	Inner City
I	Tibetan Forts	T	Outer City
J	Hunting Park	U	To Jehol (Manchuria)
K	Summer Palace (Yihoyuan)	V	Tangshan Hotsprings

of the Western Hills, changing to sombre mauves and greys in the higher, more distant peaks. Autumn is wanton in colours, particularly in the dry, crisp air of Peking. Nature calls upon all creation to conserve and save and slow down, in expectation of the approaching winter. Southerners living in Peking see the ducks fly southward and think of home.

At least once a year, the residents must be prepared for a sandstorm, which comes in May or October from the Mongolian deserts. The sky is overcast and the sun looks yellow. The dust is more like a thick layer of cloud. It gets into one's hair, ears and nose, and grits on one's teeth. Then pretty women, riding in their rickshaws, cover their faces with dainty silk shawls which stream in the wind. At home, an even coating of very fine dust covers everything. It seeps in through every crack and crevice, no matter how tightly the doors and windows are closed. The sandstorm may last for one or two days, and then the sun smiles again.

Soon, in late autumn, chrysanthemums in almost impossible variety are sold at the Lungfosy and Changtien. The crabs are fat and delicious at Chengyanglou. The bones of grass and trees grow brittle and so do those of grandfathers. The winds whistle through the pines and the date trees in the yard, changing to a keener note from the soft murmur of leaves in the summer. Summer is a memory and crickets sing on the hearth. One sweeps the front yard, but has not quite the heart to sweep away the maple leaves, and leaves a few on the steps where they have fallen.

Once more winter comes and the year's cycle is completed. The world-famous white pines of Peking (*pinus bugeanus*) stand like white, lanky ghosts on the mountains, and beggars wrapped in burlap sacks shiver in the cold.

THE CITY

GEOGRAPHICALLY, Peking is situated in the extreme northeast of the Chinese mainland, two hours by train from the port of Tientsin and one hour by train from the Great Wall in the north. The proximity of the Great Wall underlines one important historical fact. China's political centre of gravity always lay in the north. The cradle of Chinese civilization was in the Yellow River valley. The capital of the three greatest Chinese Dynasties, the Chou (1122-256 B. C.), the Han (206 B. C.—A. D. 220) and the Tang (A. D. 618-906), was in the extreme northwest, at Si-an in Shensi province. The North Sung capital, Kaifeng, was still on the bank of the Yellow River. From the thirteenth century to the present, with relatively short intervals, through the Yuan (Mongol—A. D. 1260-1367), Ming (A. D. 1368-1643), and Ching (Manchu—A. D. 1644-1911) dynasties, Peking has always been the capital of China.

The menace to Chinese civilisation had always come from the north. Geographically protected by the high Tibetan plateau and the Himalayas on the west and southwest, China had little to fear from the sea on its east and south, until in the nineteenth century western gunboats came to rule the waves. From the first millennium B. C. down to the present, this menace from the north had been ever present. In the 8th century B. C., the Chou emperors were harassed by the Shienyun (Huns) and the Jung tribes from the northwest, and the capital was moved to safety at Loyang. By the beginning of the third century B. C., the powerful Yen state, where Peking lies, had already built a long section of the Great Wall as a protection against the barbarian hordes. This mighty Yen state was among the last to be destroyed by the first Emperor of Tsin, who unified China and, by about 210 B. C., completed the Great Wall, the purpose of which was defence against the north.

Perhaps the best way to get a bird's-eye-view of the city is to stand at the top pavilion on Coal Hill just behind the palaces. This is one of the highest points in the area and close enough to the north wall to provide a full view of the whole city. Below, the colours and the grandeur of the Imperial City stretch before the eye. Its symmetrical lay-out along a central axis is unique, and contained in it is a jewel-like city within a city, its scintillating heavy golden-yellow roofs set off by the luxuriant green of the great park areas. Above the city walls with their bastions and grey parapets, the high, stately gate towers of the Inner City rise into the air two and a half miles away, while those of the Outer City, 5. An old peanut vendor. some five miles away, fade away into the thin air like a mirage. On a clear day

26

the distant walls of the Outer City may just be seen. The Outer City is often called in the local dialect Maotsecheng, or " Cap City ", for it is slightly wider from east to west and sits on the Inner City like a fitted cap. The Inner City is roughly about three miles long by three and a half miles wide, and the Inner and the Outer City combined have a circumference of about 54 li or approximately 18 miles.[1] The city walls are forty-two miles long altogether.

Seen from Coal Hill, the majestic proportions and sharply etched contours of Peking are extremely striking, only matched by its glowing colours. In the immediate foreground lies the Forbidden City with its mass of glazed, shining roofs, surrounded by yet another square of pink, crenellated walls, which delineate the Imperial City (Huangcheng). To the left in the foreground rises the graceful turret tower of the northeast corner, capped with glazed yellow and green overlapping curving roofs whose reflection can be seen in the turbid water of the moat running around the Imperial City walls. This mass of gleaming gold contrasts with the verdant foliage which surrounds it, especially luxuriant in the area of the Sea Palaces where it completely obscures the western contours of the Imperial City. From this mass of foliage rises the towering white dagoba of Peihai, and here and there one glimpses the white of the Imperial Lakes. On the right, the purple slopes of the Western Hills are an invitation to escape from the dust of the city to their temples and fresh springs. To the north lie the Shyshahai lakes and ponds covered with greenish-yellow willows and beyond them are the parks of the princes' gardens.

Coal Hill itself is a study in greens and blues. Here five pavilions are evenly distributed atop an artificial hill some 300 feet high; the middle pavilion stands on the very top and the others around and below it. Arrayed in gold, lavender and blues and greens, they are exquisite examples of pavilion structure. The central pavilion is square, with triple roofs. The next two, to its right and left on a lower level, are double-storied and hexagonal, and the lowest ones are round. We are told of Kublai Khan in the thirteenth century that " No matter how big the tree may be, he gets it carried by elephants; and in this way he has got together the most beautiful collection of trees in all the world. And he has also caused the whole hill to be covered with the ore of azure, which is very green. And thus not only are the trees all green, but the hill itself is all green likewise; and there is nothing in it that is not green; and hence it is called the 'Green Mount'; and in good sooth 'tis named well. On the top of the hill again there is a fine big palace which is all green inside and out; and thus the hill, and the trees, and the palace form a charming spectacle; and it is marvellous to see the uniformity of colour! Everybody who sees them is delighted. And the Great Khan has caused this beautiful prospect to be formed for the comfort and solace and delectation of his heart."[2] It was amidst such beauty that the last Ming Emperor, Tsungcheng, hanged himself in 1643 on a sophora tree.

Peking is divided into an Inner City and an Outer City. Western books usually refer to these as the " Tartar City " and the " Chinese City ", respectively. These are misnomers, for all Chinese records refer to them only as the Inner and Outer Cities. For centuries now, the Inner City has been more Chinese than Tartar, although at the beginning of the Manchu Dynasty it was assigned to the men of the " Eight Banners ", descendants of the soldiers who had taken part in the conquest of China. The Manchu Emperors thought it wise to have the Imperial City surrounded by Manchu descendants whose loyalty could not be questioned. The sections of the Inner City were assigned to them according to the colours of the eight banners. However, this militarily desirable scheme proved impractical, since the bannermen could not occupy the entire city and they needed the services of Chinese tradesmen. The term " Tartar City " prob-

6. Front yard of a Palace Hall, showing a sundial and incense burners.

7. The Summer Palace.

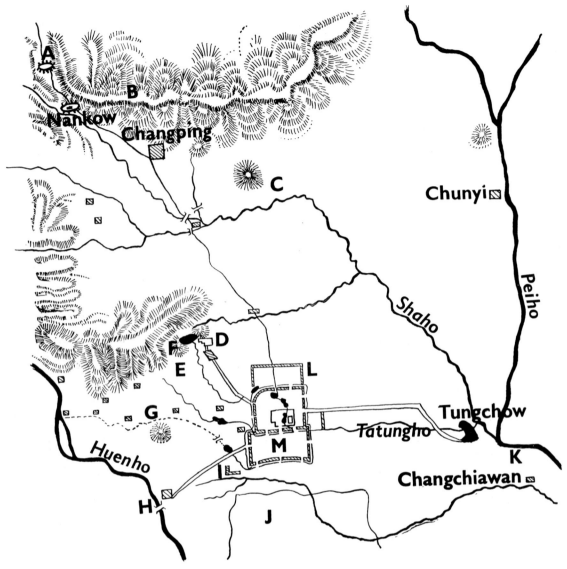

MAP OF THE ENVIRONS OF PEKING IN 1870
(AFTER BRETSCHNEIDER)

A Chuyungkuan (Pass to the Great Wall)
B Ming Tombs
C Tangshan (hot springs)
D Old Summer Palace
E New Summer Palace (not yet built)
F Jade Fountain Hill
G Old Canal
H Lukouchiao (Marco Polo Bridge)
I Chin rampart
J Nanyuan (South Park)
K Grand Canal
L Mongol rampart
M Peking

7

8
9

ably comes from Marco Polo, who often used the term, sometimes applying it indiscriminately to residents of Peking. By and large, the Manchus adopted Chinese costumes, spoke the best Pekingese and some adopted Chinese names and preferred not to be known as Manchus. Certainly they would resent being called " Tartars." In Chinese, the word " Tartar" is one of contempt. The common Chinese word for Manchus is *chijen* or " bannermen."

The population of the Inner City is overwhelmingly Chinese, although no accurate statistics are available. It is true that in the Outer City, just outside Chienmen, there is a busy district of small hotels, old temples, streets of shops selling lanterns and hats, some good and old restaurants, popular entertainment areas, and the red light district of Pata Hutung, but the bulk of business is carried on in the Inner City. It is this area that we mean when we speak of the Peking City.

In the thirteenth century, the term " Tartar City" may have been more appropriate, for Kublai Khan had commanded the Tartars to live within a mile of the city wall. At the same time he had caused the population of the Chin capital, the old Cambaluk, to move into his new city. Marco Polo strikingly describes the appearance of the suburbs in those days.

" You must know that the city of Cambaluc hath such a multitude of houses, and such a vast population inside the walls and outside, that it seems quite past all possibility. There is a suburb outside each of the gates, which are twelve in number; and these suburbs are so great that they contain more people than the city itself [for the suburb of one gate spreads in width till it meets the suburb of the next, whilst they extend in length some three or four miles].[3] In those suburbs lodge the foreign merchants and travellers, of whom there are always great numbers who have come to bring presents to the Emperor, or to sell articles at Court, or because the city affords so good a mart to attract traders. [There are in each of the suburbs, to a distance of a mile from the city, numerous fine hostelries for the lodgment of merchants from different parts of the world, and a special hostelry is assigned to each description of people, as if we should say there is one for the Lombards, another for the Germans, and a third for the Frenchmen.] And thus there are as many good houses outside of the city as inside, without counting those that belong to the great lords and barons, which are very numerous...

" Moreover, no public woman resides inside the city, but all such abide outside in the suburbs. And 'tis wonderful what a vast number of these there are for the foreigners; it is a certain fact that there are more than 20,000 of them living by prostitution. And that so many can live in this way will show you how vast is the population...

" To this city also are brought articles of greater cost and rarity, and in greater abundance of all kinds, than to any other city in the world...

" As a sample, I tell you, no day in the year passes that there do not enter the city 1000 cart-loads of silk alone, from which are made quantities of cloth of silk and gold, and of other goods. And this is not to be wondered at; for in all the countries round about there is no flax, so that everything has to be made of silk. It is true, indeed, that in some parts of the country there is cotton and hemp, but not sufficient for their wants. This, however, is not of much consequence, because silk is so abundant and cheap, and is a more valuable substance than either flax or cotton."

In Mongol times the city was larger than it is at present (see Appendix II). From Coal Hill, the old Mongol ramparts appear as a clear line of broken mud elevations about 5 li (less than two miles) to the north outside the present city wall. But the plan of a city within a city, as well as the general layout and the

8. The White Dagoba and bridge at Pei-hai.

9. Part of Ceremonial Ramp in the Forbidden City, reserved for the Emperor's sedan-chair, showing dragons in bas-relief.

33

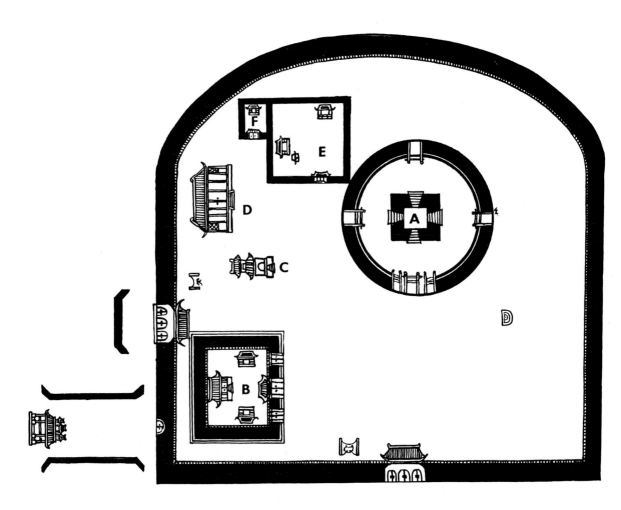

ALTAR OF THE SUN

A Altar
B Disrobing Hall
C Bell Tower
D Repository for musical instruments and other utensils
E Hall for Spirit-Tablets and Kitchen
F Slaughter House

palaces, has not changed in its essentials. On the whole, the present city with its brick walls is as the Ming Emperor Yunglo rebuilt it in A. D. 1417-1420. The plan is basically the same as that of the great Chinese capitals in ancient Si-an. Always, from earliest times, the Emperor sat in the north " facing south " and the people worshipped " facing north ", a rule as strictly observed as the Islamic law of facing towards Mecca.

Tradition and astrology influenced the conception of an imperial city. In the city of today one can see in the south the Temple of Heaven, on the north the Altar of the Earth; just outside the east gate is the Altar of the Sun, and just outside the west gate is the Terrace of the Moon. In the centre is the Polar Forbidden City (Chychincheng is often mistranslated as " Purple Forbidden City "), its name referring to the north Polar Star around which the firmaments move. The Polar City symbolizes the power of the Dragon Throne. The concept was developed and its symbolism taken seriously by the courtiers, for they believed that the influence of the stars was powerful and ever-present.

In the basic plan of the city, the main streets run north and south or east and west. Consequently it is impossible to lose one's direction in Peking, and rickshaw pullers warn those behind, not by crying the Chinese equivalent for " turning right " or " turning left," but by " *wang tung*," " *wang shi* " (" going east," " going west "). It is not easy to forget the Hatamen Boulevard which runs north and south straight as an arrow for about three miles, bounded on the south by the tall Hatamen Gate-tower, some eighty feet high, and at the other end by the Antingmen Gate-tower. The central axis is clear and unmistakable. It runs through the entire city, beginning at the Chienmen, or front south gate, running in succession through the Chunghuamen, Tienanmen, the various central gates and palaces, and ending in the Drum Tower and Bell Tower.

The grandeur of the conception comes largely from the liberal use of space. The Tienanmen Boulevard running east and west directly in front of the Forbidden City is at least 150 feet wide, and the Hatamen Boulevard at least 70 feet wide. Æsthetically, the city gives a sense of open space and serenity, rather than sublimity. Peking does not aspire; it prefers to straggle and expand, an effect which is accentuated by the low, broad and sweeping golden roofs of the palaces. A law, observed until modern times, made it illegal for any commoner's residence to have more than one storey, the idea being that no subject should be able to raise his head above the imperial palaces, or peep at a neighbour's private courtyard. Consequently, there is nothing to obstruct the open view of the sky.

This chessboard pattern and its resulting spaciousness was also characteristic of Kublai Khan's city. As Marco Polo describes it: " The streets are so straight and wide that you can see right along them from end to end and from one gate to the other. And up and down the city there are beautiful palaces, and many great and fine hostelries, and fine houses in great numbers. [All the plots of ground on which the houses of the city are built are four-square, and laid out with straight lines; all the plots being occupied by great and spacious palaces, with courts and gardens of proportionate size. All these plots were assigned to different heads of families. Each square plot is encompassed by handsome streets for traffic; and thus the whole city is arranged in squares just like a chess-board, and disposed in a manner so perfect and masterly that it is impossible to give a description that should do it justice.] "

The old city centre, as far as hotels, restaurants, shops famous for hats, furs and lanterns, and secondhand book stalls are concerned, is located in the Outer City directly outside the Chienmen Gate. The Eastern City (Inner City) is now the area of prosperous homes and important government offices, banks and hospitals. The southwest corner of the Inner City, extending to the west of the Outer City, is the oldest part and contains the greatest number of old temples and pagodas dating from the seventh to the thirteenth centuries. Some of the oldest sites, like the Poyunkuan and Tienningsy, stand directly outside the west city wall, near Shipienmen Gate. Some relatively obscure places, seldom visited by tourists, are nevertheless historically very important. The White Pagoda near the West Gate (Pingtsemen), for instance, is all that remains of the great temple where Kublai Khan himself each year, on the 15th day of the Second Month, led a procession to worship the Buddha. The area also contained many private gardens of the Manchu princes. A research scholar on the great novel *Red Chamber Dream* is of the opinion that the fabulous house-garden of the rich Chia family described in the novel was situated in the north-west corner of the city. The East

THE CITY   City contained the homes and mansions of many wealthy families, hidden away from the main Hatamen Boulevard in the quiet hutungs.

From Peking, the old metropolis, roads lead in all directions. To the southwest is the Marco Polo Bridge (Lukouchiao) some twelve miles away across the Huenho or Sangkan River (the Pulisanghin of Marco Polo). This is a strategic point, the site of many battles for the possession of the city. Here in 1937 the last Sino-Japanese War began. The Huenho comes down from the mountains in the west in a turbid torrent, and passes south of the city. In this direction lead all the railways, south toward Hankow and east toward Tientsin.

To the east, some 13 miles away, are Tungchow and its neighbouring town, Changchiawan, the terminal of the 700-mile Grand Canal connecting Peking with Hangchow below the Yangtse River. As early as the year A. D. 608, the Emperor of Sui completed the Canal, with a million conscripted workers. Three years later, in full pomp, he visited Peking via the Canal, the city then being known as Chuo District. This emperor was renowned for his love of luxury and extravagance, and his imperial barge was towed by three teams of seventy to eighty palace maidens, each team dressed in a different colour. It is interesting to note that when in the 1860's Lord Macartney came to Peking in his "embassy boat", at Tungchow the boat was lifted across a canal lock. A photograph[4] shows that the boat was held up by ropes controlled from a pair of capstans high on both banks. Before the Tientsin-Pukow Railway was completed, Chinese

10. View of the Lama Temple.

11. Part of the Forbidden City.

officials and their families coming to Peking used to travel by boat up the Canal, get off at Tungchow, and enter Peking by the East Gate. This, the longest canal in the world, was the great waterway from the south of China just as the Lu-kouchiao route on the east was the land route.

The West Gate used to mark the beginning of the road leading out into the western suburbs. It is the oldest, untouched gate, and in the immediate area of the gate tower it still retains the characteristics of the ancient gates, with streets and markets leading immediately from the gate-yard to the suburb. Since a great stone-paved road has been built at Shichymen on the north-west corner, providing a good route to the Summer Palace at the foot of the Western Hills, the West Gate has diminished in importance.

On the north, beyond the Altar of the Earth outside the Antingmen Gate, the route leads through Chunyi district to the pass in the Great Wall known as the Kupeikow, and beyond Jehol and other points in Manchuria. On the west side of the north wall, the Tehshengmen leads thirty miles to the north through Changping district and thence directly to the Ming Tombs and, a little to the west of these, to the famous historic Chuyungkuan pass in the Great Wall. It connects with Kalgan in Inner Mongolia and also with the area of the famous stone sculptures of Tatung in the neighbouring province of Shensi.

The western suburb is the great pleasure ground. Here stand the Summer Palace (Yihoyuan), built by the Empress Dowager in 1894, the old Summer Palace (Yuanmingyuan, the residences of the great Emperors Kangshi and Chien-lung, destroyed by English and French troops in 1860), and other princes' homes. The southwestern corner is the Fengtai district, known for its flowers. In this region are extensive marshy areas which the Ming Emperor Yunglo fenced off from the public and used as private hunting grounds. The southeastern corner is quiet and completely rural. The northwest suburb once had an important canal system used for transporting soldiers, and historical records tell of military vessels from the north using it. An extensive reservoir area is situated in the northwestern corner of the city. When Emperor Hungwu rebuilt the city the reservoir was cut in two, one half remaining outside the present city wall and the other half, the Chishuitan, just inside the Tehshengmen Gate. Here Prince Chun and a few other Manchu princes had their residences. The lakes and ponds which lead from the reservoirs give this whole northwest corner of the city a more rural aspect than the rest of the city. These in turn lead through the three large lake areas of Shyshahai (front, central and rear) to the Sea Palaces and then become the River of Golden Water (Chinshuiho) which crosses the Taihomen yard in front of the palaces. The general direction of the water system is from north-west to southeast. It starts from the Jade Fountain and then, at the north-western corner, divides into two streams which feed the moats around the city, one going east and south and the other along the west wall. It then turns east along the south wall and the two join up again near Tungpienmen and flow into the Tatung River leading to Tungchow.

A further word must be said about the Shyshahai area, for it is particularly in this northwestern quarter of the city that the scene is rustic and one has the impression of living in the country. Trees and lotus-covered lakes and willow-bordered embankments abound. This is the great area for relaxation in summer. In the late afternoons young college students and girls saunter under the generous shade and sip *suanmeitang*, a delicious cold drink made of wild plums. The rhythmic clanging of the copper saucers of the men who sell this fruit juice can be heard along its embankments, while at night oil burners throwing off big clouds of black smoke illuminate the throngs of pedlars and holiday-makers along the paths.

12. Part of the Painted Gallery at the Summer Palace.

ANCIENT GLORY

PEKING, the capital of China since the time of the Norman Conquest of England, is both a reminder of ancient glory and a living testimony to the men who have created it. The miles of massive grey walls, with their bastions and parapets impart a sense of strength and antiquity—something defiant of time. Apart from the imperial palaces of Tokyo, nothing in the world so stimulates the mind and evokes visions of ancient oriental glory and power. Even as the train from Tientsin approaches the city, running at an angle to the city wall, the massive projecting bastions, gun turrets and moats and the eighty-foot-high gate towers sweep rapidly by, in unforgettable grandeur, evoking a sense of wonder. Peking seems ageless, and, for a moment, all remembrance of western civilization is forgotten. Peking stretches before one as the materialization of a mediaeval dream.

What historical associations it has! Two emperors of the Northern Sung were captured alive and brought here in the beginning of the twelfth century by the Nüchen chieftains of Chin; Jenghiz Khan's captains assaulted the walls from the west and north and, after some fifty years, his grandson, Kublai Khan, built the new Khambalik (Cambaluk, Cambaluc) on the present site and made it the capital of a vast empire which extended to the Black Sea. Here at the East Gate, the Chinese soldiers of the first Ming Emperor, under their Commander-in-chief Shü Ta, threw a temporary bridge across the moat, scaled the walls of the East Gate, and drove out the last Mongol ruler who, together with his concubines, made a hasty flight from the Sea Palaces which his grandfathers had created.

This happened in the 14th century, but already the Peking area was rich in historical associations. According to legend, as early as the latter part of the twenty-third century, B. C., Emperor Shun (2255-2206 B. C.) exiled to Yuchow the families of four wicked ministers who had been giving him trouble. Ancient geography places this Yuchow 38 li, or approximately 12 miles, northwest of Changping, which would bring it in the region of the Chuyungkuan pass beyond the Great Wall. At the beginning of the Chou Dynasty, about 1122 B. C., Emperor Wu is said to have settled the descendants of Huangti (Yellow Emperor) in this region.[5] Looking northwest, where the Mongol rampart turns south, about one mile outside the northwest gate of the present city, stands a Huangting (" royal pavilion ") which contains an inscription by Emperor Chienlung marking the site of one of the gates of the city Chi, the ancient capital of Yen State. From the second century B. C. through the Han and the Tang dynasties, with various interludes of rebellion and independence, this region continued to be a principality, the holdings of a prince of Yen. To this day a classic name for Peking is Yenching ("Yen capital"). In Ming times this northwest region was a great park area, covered with old trees, which have now completely disappeared.

During the fourth, fifth and sixth centuries A. D., the whole of North China was occupied by five Hu barbarian tribes, whose peoples slowly settled down and intermarried with the Chinese, bringing fresh blood to the old Chinese race. The richer Chinese families moved south, establishing around Nanking a centre of the arts, fine living, and art criticism.[6]

It was in Peking that An Lushan, of Tartar extraction, who called himself the King of Yen, raised a rebellion in the eighth century against the Tang Dynasty to capture the tragic and extravagant queen Yang Kweifei, and forced the flight of the Tang Emperor Minghuang to Szechuen (see *ill.* 57). The Tang house never quite recovered its power after An Lushan's rebellion.

After the fall of the Tang Dynasty, the Liaos (a Khitan tribe) captured Peking in A. D. 936-7, and called it "Nanking" or Southern Capital, to distinguish it from its northern capital in Liaotung (Manchuria). They held it until A. D. 1122 when yet another northern tribe, the Nüchens, who were related to the Manchus, captured it and returned it to the Sung. Only three years later, the same Nüchens overthrew the North Sung Dynasty and forced it to establish its capital in the south at Hangchow. During the whole of the South Sung Dynasty (A. D. 1127-1279), North China was lost to the Nüchen Chins (also spelled as Kins in sinological works). Thus it was under the Liaos and the Chins that Peking became a national capital.

In 1211-15, the Mongols under Jenghiz Khan's general repeatedly attacked and finally took the city from the Chins, while Jenghiz himself, in his drive for world conquest, continued toward the Caspian and the Black Sea. In 1234, ten years after Jenghiz Khan's death, the Chin state was destroyed. War and turmoil continued in Inner Mongolia and Turkestan until Kublai Khan mounted the throne in 1260. Under the Chins, Peking had already become a great and prosperous capital city. Kublai made it his capital in 1264 even before he had subjugated the rest of China.

Thus Peking acquired different names through the centuries. Some of them persist in literature to this day.

Before the tenth century: Yenching (Capital of Yen); city named Chi; also Yuchow.
Liao .... Yenching, later Nanking (South Capital).
Chin .... Chungtu (Central Capital).
Mongol .... Tatu (Great Capital), or Khambalik.
Ming .... Peiping (Northern Peace).
After 1403 (Ming) ..... Peking (Peiching, North Capital).

The city varied in size and site in the different periods. An enormous amount of research has been done and a great many facts have been assembled, particularly in a work called *Jyshia*, to determine the changes in the history of Peking.

This book was undertaken by one man, Chu Yichun (A. D. 1629-1709),[7] the great scholar and friend of Emperor Kangshi. The work was regarded as so important that Emperor Chienlung appointed a board of editors to verify and revise it and add any material which Chu might have overlooked.[8]

Many western scholars have devoted themselves to the study of the history of Peking, among them Father Hyacinthe Bitchurin, Dr. Bretschneider, Father Favier, and Osvald Sirén.[9] Bretschneider provided European scholars with the basic information. He was fully and accurately informed from Chinese sources, and made accurate maps of the sites. Unfortunately Father Favier drew some untenable conclusions about the site of the Chin capital, which have had considerable influence on later scholars. His map was reproduced in Juliet Bredon's *Peking*, Arlington and Lewisohn's *In Search of Old Peking*, and Maurice Fabre's *Pékin*. It is time that his error was corrected (see Appendix III).

The size of Chi cannot be accurately determined. There is no adequate evidence to indicate that the east and west walls of the present city were not identical with those of the Mongol city. The exact southern limit of the Mongol city is open to some question (see Appendix II). In spite of the fact that Emperor Yunglo officially changed the names of the gates, the people still call them by the names given to them in Mongol times. This is particularly true of the gate popularly known as Hatamen, which goes back to the Mongol period when it was near the garden of Prince Hata. The outside limits of the Chin capital cannot be accurately determined. Certainly the palaces of the Chins were not where Favier thought they should be (see Appendix III).

In general, the present city may be said to date from around 1270, and was built by Kublai Khan. When the Mings defeated the Mongols about a hundred years later, in 1368, the first emperor greatly extended and modified it. It reached its glory under Emperor Yunglo in the first half of the fifteenth century. Just as the Chins had employed Chinese architects from the conquered Chinese capital and built their palaces according to its designs, so Yunglo rebuilt his palaces and temples and residences on the model of Nanking, "only on a grander and more beautiful scale."[10] Succeeding emperors continuously strengthened and improved the city, and Emperor Chiatsing in 1553 added the walls of the Outer City, as they stand now.

The repairs and renovations continued till 1564 (see Appendix I). Eighty years later, the last of the Ming emperors hanged himself, and the Manchus took over. The Manchu emperors Kangshi and Chienlung did not change the pattern of the palaces or the city itself, but devoted themselves to beautifying and adorning its temples and palaces, both in the city and in the adjoining Western Hills.

Outside the southwest corner of the city, near Poyunkuan in the neighbourhood of the race course, is a series of mud ramparts which date back to the tenth and eleventh centuries. Still farther out, some eight li (three li approximately equal one mile) from the southwestern corner of the present Outer City, is a more extended rampart of the old Chin capital dating back to the twelfth century which includes a section of its southwestern corner. These are the earliest ancient remains of the old site of Peking, older than the Mongol ramparts beyond the north wall of the Inner City (see Appendix III).

Ample evidence exists to prove that throughout the Tang and Sung periods (i. e. from the seventh to the thirteenth centuries), the capital was situated outside the present Inner City, on its southwestern corner. It included a narrow strip of the western side of the Outer City and, with the exception of the Summer Palace of the Chin capital, it was separated from the Inner City.

Kublai Khan built his city to the northeast of the Chin capital. This distance between the present and the ancient city is variously given as three li in the official *Mongol History*, half a mile by Odoric, "contiguous" by Rachid-eddin, the Persian historiographer, and as "separated only by a river" by Marco Polo.

This river is today the Sanliho, running from the west into the moat around the southwest corner of the Inner City. In ancient history it was known as the Canal of Queen Shiao of the Liao Dynasty. Queen Shiao was a notable woman, celebrated in history for her strength of character. Since the seventh century, the

13. The Tower of Buddha's Fragrance at the Summer Palace.

42

14

15

Grand Canal came up to Tungchow, about thirteen miles east of Peking, and this queen had the river opened to connect with the Tatungho on the east leading to Tungchow. In the beginning of the twelfth century there was strong pressure from the northern Chin hordes on both the Liaos in Peking and on the Sungs in Kaifeng. Threatened by the Chins in the north, the Liao queen sought an understanding with the Sung. In 1112, one of her Chinese generals, Kuo, with 8,000 of his troops, defected and went over to the Chinese side. In October, the Chinese army established its base some ten miles southwest of the Liao capital at what is today called Marco Polo Bridge (Lukouchiao). In the night, Kuo led his troops silently across the river, each soldier biting a piece of wood in his mouth so that none would make any noise.

The next morning 5,000 troops mixed with the peasants and entered the south gate in disguise, fought their way to Minchungsy Temple (today called the Fayuansy), and demanded the queen's surrender. She refused and the battle raged into the night. Then her reinforcements arrived and Kuo escaped with barely a few hundred soldiers by jumping from the city wall. The Sung campaign was called off.

Meanwhile the Chin general Akuta was poised in the mountains to the north, at Chuyungkuan. When he heard that the Sung had been defeated, he descended upon the Peking plains. The famous Queen Shiao fled, the city surrendered, and the Liao dynasty came to an end.

Between 1113 and 1115 the Chins returned the city to the Sung and the latter insisted on calling Peking officially a "district city", known as Yenshanfu. In 1115, the Chin Dynasty really began, and eleven years later they conquered the Chinese capital, Kaifeng. The Sung Emperor Huitsung and his son were captured and taken north. The invaders looted the treasures of Kaifeng and took Chinese architects to rebuild and beautify Peking.

Under the Chins, Peking was known as "Chungtu" and was the capital of North China, growing rapidly in size and importance.

It already had an outer wall, "measuring seventy-five li," or roughly twenty-three miles round, situated to the southwest of the present city.[11]

Princes and princesses occupied fine residences both in the city and in the outskirts. Particularly beautiful was the present Peihai (North Sea) area within Imperial City where the Chin Lords had their summer palaces. It was then called the Emerald Isle (Chiunghuatao). There the *chuangtai* (ladies' chamber) of the witty and beautiful imperial concubine Li of Changtsung (A. D. 1190-1208) was located. It was she who, seeing the vicissitudes of fortune, said of the imperial treasures, "Owners are not necessarily their keepers, and keepers are not necessarily their owners."

The *Hailing Chi* says that "the greater part of the interior of Yen City was taken up by forbidden areas, and there were very few civilian residences there. The grandeur of its palaces, its intricate, winding walls extending in all directions and reaching skyward lost nothing by comparison with the Opang Palaces of the Tsin or the Chienchang of the Han. On the day I was received in audience, when I went to Yenshan on an official mission, I saw the magnificence of his royal guards, which exceeded that of the Chinese capital. His imperial throne was inlaid with seven kinds of jewels. On both sides were two lions over ten feet high. Liang, the Chin ruler [i. e., Prince of Hailing], had a dark, black complexion and a long beard and his eyes looked downward. I saw him in person at the Tsengyuan Hall."

During the period when the Chins tolerated the Southern Sung Dynasty as a tributary power, Sung emissaries made many dutiful journeys to Chungtu to offer congratulations on Imperial birthdays and other state occasions. Many

14. The Ming Dynasty bas-relief of the Nine Dragons at the Winter Palace.

15. A doorway in the residential section of the Winter Palace.

45

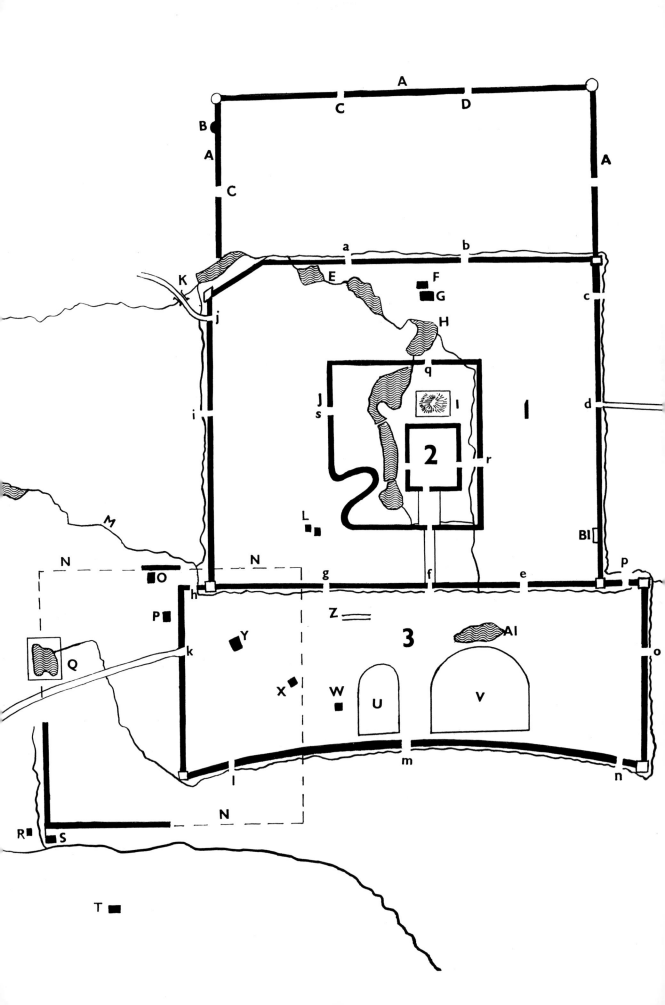

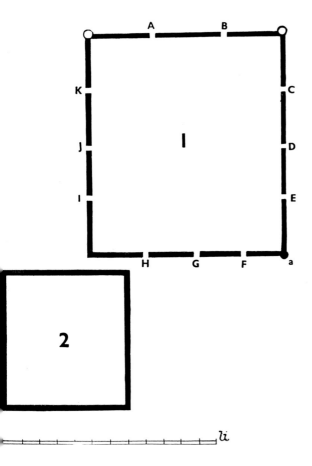

THE MONGOL CITY OF PEKING
(AFTER BRETSCHNEIDER)

1 City of Great Khan,
Mongol (Yuan) Dynasty
A Chientehmen
B Antsengmen
C Kwangshimen
D Tsungjenmen
E Chihuamen
F Wenmingmen
G Lichengmen
H Shunchengmen
I Pingtsemen
J Hoyimen
K Shuchingmen

According to Bretschneider the Mongol city was 50 li around (11.64 li east to west, and less than 13 li north to south). Chinese records give 60 li as the measurements. (14 li=5 miles.)

2 Chin Capital
This map by Bretschneider gives the city circumference as 28 li (4×7 li) and therefore represents the size of the Tang City Yuchow.

MODERN PEKING (MAP AFTER BRETSCHNEIDER)

AAA Mongol Rampart
B Royal Pavilion marks a gate of the ancient city of Chi
C West Little Pass
D East Little Pass
E Tsishuitan
F Bell Tower
G Drum Tower
H Shyshahai
I Coal Hill
J Madame Pien's Tomb
K Kaoliang's Bridge
L Double Pagoda Temple
M Sanliho
NN Imaginary line of Chin Inner City
O Poyunkuan
P Tienningsy
Q Lotus Pond

R Black Public Cemetery
S Ofangying
T Liuchun
U Temple of Agriculture
V Temple of Heaven
W Heiyaochang
X Fayuansy
Y Tutimiao
Z Liulichang
A1 Goldfish Pond
B1 Observatory
C1 To Tungchow
D1 Ancient Rampart (period not determined)
a Tehshengmen
b Antingmen
c Tungchymen
d Chihuamen

e Hatamen
f Chienmen
g Shüanwumen
h Shipienmen
i Pingtsemen
j Shichymen
k Changyimen
l Yu-anmen or Nanshimen
m Yungtingmen
n Tsoanmen
o Shawomen
p Tungpienmien
q Houmen
r Tunganmen
s Shianmen
1 Inner City
2 Forbidden City
3 Outer City

contemporaneous Chinese records exist to tell of the splendour of the Chin court. Fan Chengta (A. D. 1126-1193), a high official and an inveterate traveller, provides a personal impression of the court.[12]

"Soon I entered Shüanming Gate. Inside the gate stood over two hundred guards, wearing gold-sprinkled double-phoenix turbans and flowery red brocade jackets. They were standing at ease. I went into the *Jenhotien* [audience hall]. The big carpet in phoenix design before the entrance covered half the yard. On both sides were wing structures, two storeys high, called the East and West towers. The corridors around these towers were covered with screens, and guards in armour stood along the wall.

"Those on the east wore red felt armour and held spears wound round with gold thread; their yellow banner was painted with a green dragon. Those on the west wore blue felt armour and carried spears wound round with gold thread; their white banner carried the picture of a yellow dragon. These guards lined up right to the entrance of the hall, but the guards at the main door wore brocade over-jackets and carried bows and arrows. On both sides of the steps leading to the entrance were displayed insignia and parasols, such as we see at the mass of Taoist priests. An officer took me up by the eastern flight of steps, then turning north, I entered the hall from the terrace...

"The lord of the Chins wore a turban and a red gown, with a jade belt. He was sitting on the seven-jewelled throne, on both sides of which was a large screen showing dragons in water. On all sides, the walls were hung with tapestries of embroidered dragons, and the beams and girders were clothed in embroidery. Between the two railings, the space was furnished with golden lions, *man* carpets, mats for Buddhist worship, and scented with Tachu perfumes. On both sides stood fourteen or fifteen officers wearing jade belts and golden fish, or gold belts [insignia of rank], facing each other and looking straight ahead.

"There were innumerable palace structures in front and behind, extravagant beyond measure and built with infinite artistry. The Yang Prince [named] Liang, had these built according to the design of Kung Yenchou. A total of 800,000 conscript labourers and 400,000 soldiers were engaged on it. It took them several years and those who died were without number. The windows, screens and partitions used in the building of the palaces of the north capital were all taken from Pienliang [North Sung Capital, Kaifeng]. Among the architects of Pienliang, there was one whose name was Yen Yung [meaning 'Yen Employed']. He was a great artist and all his works bore his signature. When he was employed at Yen, it was recognized that his name already foretold what he was going to do."

The Chins were swept away by the Mongols, the most devastating of all the Northern invaders. Jenghiz Khan had ruled from Karakoram, west of Urga. However, Kublai Khan was crowned in Shangtu, near Dolon-Nor, directly north across the Great Wall, and much nearer to Peking. He decided to build his new capital on the foundations of the great Chin capital. The rich Chinese empire to the south, with its culture and civilization, was an irresistible attraction to a man of his calibre. It contrasted pleasantly with the Mongolian wilds, the Turkestan and Pamir plateaus and barren Tibet. The tranquillity of the Chinese people may well have attracted him, and he had ambitions to found a peaceful empire. He could not help admiring the Chinese Great Wall, covering 1,800 miles, built in the third century B. C., and the Grand Canal, completed around A. D. 600, which connected Peking with Hangchow. The vast empire inherited from his grandfather, Jenghiz Khan, was almost disintegrating from its own size. Nevertheless the momentum of Mongol military power was so great that even after Jenghiz died, it carried war and destruction as far as the Black

16. Detail of some of the Thousand Buddhas on the walls of the Winter Palace.

17. Detail of the bas-relief of the Nine Dragons at the Winter Palace.

Sea and the Carpathian Mountains, laying waste every area it touched. One
of Kublai's grand-nephews, for instance, was King of Persia, when Marco Polo
decided to return to Venice. Being a comparatively civilized man, Kublai Khan
appreciated the culture and institutions of China as he found them. But Shangtu
beyond the Great Wall was difficult to reach and inconvenient for audiences with
emissaries from the entire Asiatic continent. He remained loyal to the Mongolian nomad life of horses, tents, and mares' milk (he had some Mongolian desert
plants growing in the royal yards of Peking), but he started to rebuild Peking
between the years 1264-1267. In 1272 he named it Tatu (Marco Polo's Kambaluk),
which means the " Great Capital " in Chinese. He still passed his spring and
summer months at Shangtu (the " Upper Capital ") but when the desert grass
began to brown, he came to Peking for the winter.

Already in his childhood his grandfather had appreciated Kublai's intelligence
and told his people to heed what he said. Having " a becoming amount of
flesh," and " very shapely in all his limbs," he was of good stature, " neither tall
nor short, but of a middle height." Marco Polo records that " his complexion
is white and red, the eyes black and fine, the nose well formed and well set
on. He has four wives, whom he retains permanently as his legitimate consorts;
...And each of them has a special court of her own, very grand and ample; no

51

one of them having fewer than 300 fair and charming damsels. They have also many pages and eunuchs, and a number of other attendants of both sexes; so that each of these ladies has not less than 10,000 persons attached to her court."[13]

Marco Polo has left us a graphic description of the magnificence and grandeur of the Peking of his days. No doubt he greatly admired Kublai Khan, who was a civilized man appreciative of the amenities of life, and Marco was young (he was twenty-one when he arrived), observant, pleasant, and had a certain shrewdness inherent in the Polo family of traders. He tells us, " You must know that it is the Greatest Palace that ever was." " The Hall of the Palace is so large that it could easily dine 6,000 people; and it is quite a marvel to see how many rooms there are besides. The building is altogether so vast, so rich and so beautiful, that no man on earth could design anything superior to it. The outside of the roof also is all colours with vermilion and yellow and green and blue and other hues, which are fixed with a varnish so fine and exquisite that they shine like crystal, and lend a resplendent lustre to the Palace as seen for a great way round."

His description of the Khan's great dining hall, where the ladies sat with the men, a most un-Chinese custom, is particularly charming.

" And when the Great Khan sits at table on any great court occasion, it is in this fashion. His table is elevated a good deal above the others, and he sits at the north end of the hall, looking towards the south, with his chief wife beside him on the left. On his right sit his sons and his nephews, and other kinsmen of the Blood Imperial, but lower, so that their heads are on a level with the Emperor's feet. And then the other Barons sit at other tables lower still. So also with the women; for all the wives of the Lord's sons, and of his nephews and other kinsmen, sit at the lower table to his right, and below them again the ladies of the other Barons and Knights, each in the place assigned by the Lord's orders. The tables are so disposed that the Emperor can see the whole of them from end to end, many as they are.....

" In a certain part of the hall near where the Great Khan holds his table, there [is set a large and very beautiful piece of workmanship in the form of a square coffer, or buffet, about three paces each way, exquisitely wrought with figures of animals finely carved and gilt. The middle is hollow, and in it] stands a great vessel of pure gold, holding as much as an ordinary butt; and at each corner of the great vessel is one of smaller size [of the capacity of a firkin], and from the former the wine or beverage flavoured with fine and costly spices is drawn off into the latter..... The value of these pitchers and cups is something immense; in fact, the Great Khan has such a quantity of this kind of plate, and of gold and silver in other shapes, as no one ever before saw or heard tell of, or could believe.....

" At every door of the hall (or, indeed, wherever the Emperor may be) there stand a couple of big men like giants, one on each side, armed with staves. Their business is to see that no one steps upon the threshold in entering, and if this does happen, they strip the offender of his clothes, and he must pay a forfeit to have them back again; or in lieu of taking his clothes, they give him a certain number of blows.....

" They have the mouth and nose muffled with fine napkins of silk and gold, so that no breath nor odour from their persons should taint the dish or the goblet presented to the Lord. And when the Emperor is going to drink, all the musical instruments, of which he has vast store of every kind, begin to play. And when he takes the cup all the Barons and the rest of the company drop on their knees and make the deepest obeisance before him, and then the Emperor doth drink. But each time that he does so the whole ceremony is repeated.....

" But you should know that in every case where a Baron or Knight dines at those tables, their wives also dine there with the other ladies. And when all have

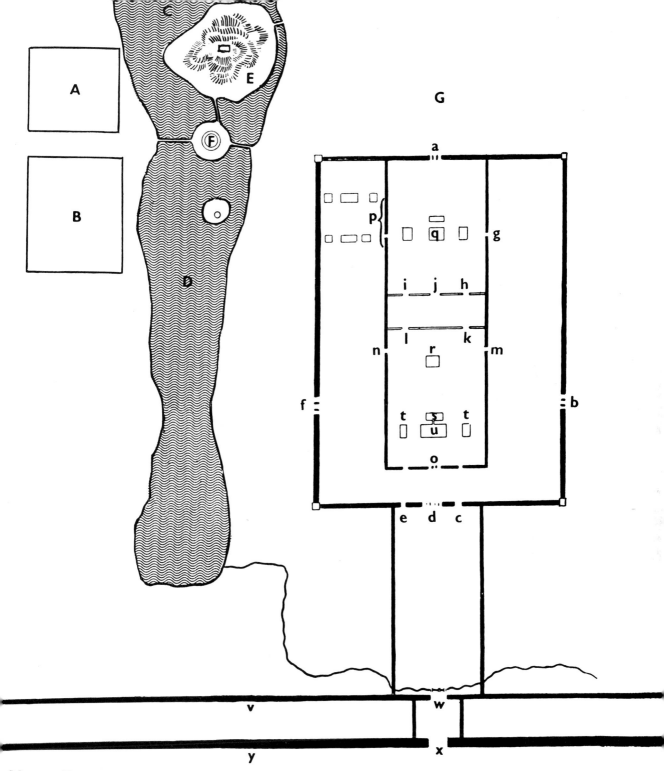

MONGOL PALACE

A Shingsheng Kung B Lungfokung C Taiyichy D Haitse E Chiunghuatao F Round City G Lingyu Park a Houtsaimen b Tunghuamem c Shingkungmen d Tsungtienmen e Yungtsungmen f Tsytantien g Chingyaomen h Yifanmen i Chiatsemen j Yenchunmen k Chiachingmen l Chingfomen m Fengyimen n Linjuimen o Tamingmen p Inner Palace q Yenchunko r Paoyutien s Hsiangko tt Wensytien u Tamingtien (Throne Hall) v Queen Shiao's Rampart (Liao) w Lingshingmen x Lichengmen y South Wall of Khanbaligh

53

dined and the tables have been removed, then come in a great number of players and jugglers, adepts at all sorts of wonderful feats, and perform before the Emperor and the rest of the company, creating great diversion and mirth, so that everybody is full of laughter and enjoyment."[14]

The clearest description of the throne room was given by Shiao Shün. His valuable *Kukung Yilu* is an account of the palaces in consecutive order. Shiao was a secretary of the Ministry of Public Works at the beginning of the régime when Emperor Hungwu had driven out the Mongols and he was sent up with a high official to examine the palaces.

"The Tamingtien is the throne hall, used also for coronations, and New Year and birthday celebrations. It has eleven *chien* [a term of house measurement]. 200 feet wide, 120 feet deep, and 90 feet high. The surrounding gallery is 7 *chien*, 240 feet deep, 44 feet wide and 50 feet high. The bedroom is 5 *chien*, with two rooms on both sides of 5 *chien*. At the back it is connected with the Shiangko [perfume hall]. The bases of the columns are in green peppered stone, and the upper pediments of alabaster and the surrounding railing is of fine-grained stone. The floor is covered with double carpets. The red beams are painted with gold, with carved dragons on them. On all sides are red carved windows bordered with rings. The ceiling is painted in gold and decorated. The double flight of steps are in marble and the red balustrades, are gilded. Under a copper flying eagle is placed the seven-jewelled imperial throne in designs of clouds and dragons. The throne has a white cover and a cushion of cloth of gold."

The author mentions an important fact, that with the Mongol rulers a seat was always provided for the empress.

It is not necessary here to describe in detail the rear palaces, the library, the ancestral temple, the provisions for pleasure in the Mongol capital, all of which are minutely described by Tao Tsungyi of the fourteenth century in his *Chuokenglu*. But some idea may be given of the riches and architectural thought and skill which went into the construction of Wanshuishan and the Haitse. These correspond to the present Sea Palaces area and formed the core of the Yuan imperial pleasure grounds. At the back of the palace near the Houtsaimen, which is the Houmen, or Back Gate today, were high towers overlooking the city, where the Yuan rulers were entertained by their palace dancers. Further down and toward the west, was the bath, and a side door led to the "Haitse" lake area, which, according to the records, was five or six li wide, or approximately two miles.

We are told, in the 14,000-word-long description in *Kukung Yilu* by Shiao Shün, that "a flying bridge rises over the middle of the lake connecting with the Yingchow Yuantien (the Tuancheng or Round City of today). A stone city wall surrounds it. Different small islets are formed, connected by arched bridges, enabling the pleasure boats of dragon design to pass under them. From the back of the Yingchowtien, the long bridge leads northwards toward the Wanshuishan." (This was the name given in Yuan times to the big island in the North Sea, where the White Dagoba now stands.) "The Wanshuishan Hill is several hundred feet high. It is full of rocks of rare quality and shapes, forming rockeries to fit in with the landscape. A stone gateway with three gates directly faces the Yingchow on the south. On its east is the Taiyi Lake and on the northwest it looks over the Haitse. Different paths lead from this stone gateway up the east and the west side. Halfway up is the site of an old temple, which contains the stone terrace where the Chin rulers used to play chess."

Shiao describes how one goes up past the Fanghutien, hidden behind a park area of tall, shady pines and cypresses; the Lukung Cave, the Chinlutien (Golden Dew Hall), and the Yuhungtien (Jade Rainbow Hall). These two halls lead by connecting paths to the Kwanghantien (Moon Palace) at the top. "The Moon

19. A gate-tower in the wall of the Inner (Tartar) City.

20. 'The Kirghizes presenting horses to Chienlung': a scroll by the eighteenth century Jesuit priest Castiglione, known in Chinese as Lang Shih-ning.

54

20

Palace is decorated with gold and pearls and circular windows and is provided with gold beds. It measures twelve beams; the walls are covered with dragons and clouds in bas-relief, and painted with yellow gold. On the side and at the back, an intricately carved wainscoting of sandalwood, in the form of clouds, consisting of thousands and tens of thousands of small pieces, goes up toward the ceiling where again lies a gold painted dragon..... A terrace stands on the outside, surrounded with a white stone balustrade. Near this point is an iron pole several dozen feet high, on top of which are suspended three gourds of gold. These are tied down with an iron chain and were put there by Emperor Chang-tsung [husband of the famous Imperial Concubine Li of the Chin Dynasty], for the purpose of subjugating the spirit in the dragon pool below. Leaning on the balustrade, one has a completely unobstructed view, with the Yingchowtien and the three palaces and their shining golden roofs in front, while at the back one sees the clouds over the Western Hills and the mass of green foliage leading toward the city gates. The waves glitter in circles and the sky seems to come down to meet them. One cannot help feeling transported away from this world.

" On the left of the hill, going down several dozen steps, is a bath, hidden among thousands of willow trees. In front of the bath is a small hall. One reaches the bath by going round this hall. There are nine rooms in the bath, which are

Crossbows

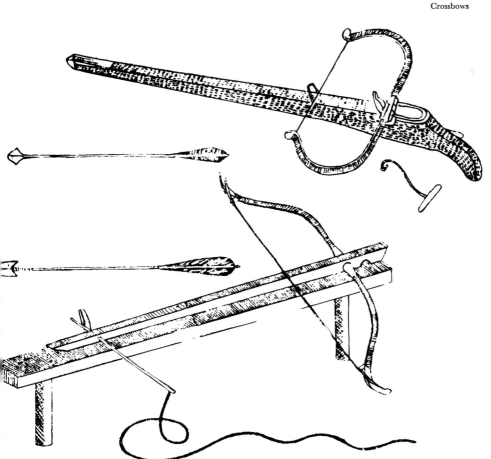

21. General view of the Great Wall at Nankow.

59

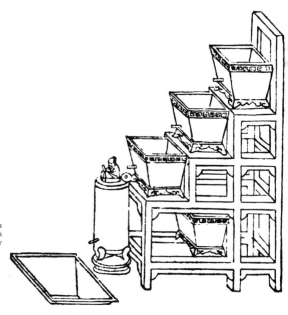

Water clock. The water vessels flow into each other, the figure at the bottom moving with the varying level telling the hour... filled every twenty-four hours.

quite bright and are built into the rocks. One can lose one's way there. A dragon rears its head over the middle cave, spurting a flow of warm water into the nine rooms, a ball rotating in its mouth. All the nine rooms are then filled with foaming water, and the fragrant steam comes out from the dragon's mouth. It is indeed a work of rare ingenuity....."

" Crossing over to the west bank, one comes upon the area famous mainly for the Shingshengtien and the Lungfokung. Here the artifice which goes into the architecture and the planning of baths, ladies' chambers, the library and the animal parks, is on a par with those on the east. Three or four li out is a dragon boat about a hundred feet long, covered with red silk festoons. When the dragon's head moves, all the internal parts move with it. A few other boats lie about, all exquisitely made. It seems eminently a good place to lose oneself and forget the outside world. Behind the new hall two round crystal buildings made entirely of glass rise from the water. When the sun shines upon them, the reflections make them appear like an underwater palace. A long bridge leads to a long, broad path into the Chishitien; two perpendicular pieces of rock, twenty feet high and only just over a foot wide, stand at the head of the bridge, hung over with golden silks shining in the sun. Across a lawn of flowers, one enters the

Muskets

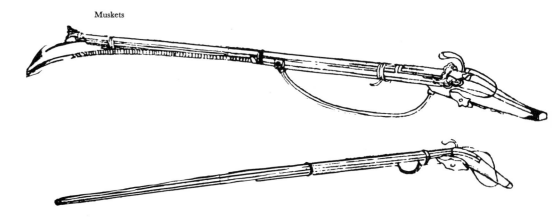

60

Yitehtien which has a complete set of corridors and bedrooms as in the main palaces. This is the place where the Mongol lord first sat when he made Peking his capital....."

From the historical records, it is clear there were many fascinating mechanical devices in use in Peking at this time; the lions and the dragon in the dragon boat were provided with internal mechanisms; a mill at Peihai was worked neither by man power nor by animals, and a system was provided for pumping the water from the Chinshuiho up to the summit at the Moon Palace. The water clock at the Tamingtien is particularly interesting and there are four or five references concerning it. Shiao Shün describes the clock, or klepsydra, as follows:

" Here was a *tenglou* [*lou* means drip; an hourglass is called *shalou*, or sand drip]. It is run by water power by a mechanism.

" Small figures holding a wooden tablet [indicating the time] in their hands come out to signal the hours and quarter hours. It is made of wood, but painted silver on the inside and lacquered. It is engraved with the curving shape of a golden dragon and clouds. It is 15 feet high, and has a capacity of over 60 *shy* (a liquid and dry measure)."

The *Yuan History* describes this mechanism in more detail. " The construction of the *tenglou* at the Tamingtien is as follows. It has a seventeen-foot framework made of gold. Above a cross-bar is a ball, with a sun on its left and a moon on its right. Below this ball is another ball. On both ends of the cross-bar is a dragon's head, with open mouth and movable eyes, which tells the speed of flow of the water. On a middle bar is a pair of dragons playing with a pearl, which float up and down according to the level of the water. The round lamp itself is variously decorated with gold and jewels. It is divided into four storeys on the inside, with four gods turning round, indicating the positions of the sun, the moon and the constellations. It makes one revolution towards the left once a day. On the next level, are figures of a dragon, a tiger, a bird and a turtle, each in its proper position; each one jumps and strikes a bell according to its quarter, in response to the mechanism inside. On the next level down the ball is calibrated into a hundred degrees, over which are indicated the twelve *chen* (two-hour periods). At each *chen* a figure carrying an hour tablet comes out to indicate the hour. Another figure at the door holds a hand steadily pointing to the quarter. Below, on the four corners, are four figures holding respectively a bell, a drum, a *cheng* and a *jao* [smaller bells without a tongue]. The bell is sounded at the first quarter, the drum at the second, the *cheng* at the third and the *jao* at the fourth..... Its mechanism is concealed in the box and is moved by water."

The *Shu Tsychy Tungchien* gives a description of other similar mechanisms:

" In the fourteenth year of Chycheng of the Yuan period [i. e. A. D. 1354] Emperor Shunti had a dragon boat built, 120 feet long and 20 feet high. Twenty-four boatmen, dressed in gold and purple, are employed moving the boat between the rear palaces and the front palaces, around the hill on the lake on pleasure trips. When the boat moves, the dragon's head, eyes and mouth, and his claws and tail all move. Again, he had a palace hour-drip made, six or seven inches [*sic!*] high, and half as wide. A box of wood conceals a jar where water moves up and down. On top of the box is a temple of the Three Holy Ones, and on its side stand *yünu* [" jade damsels," i. e., angels], each holding a tablet indicating the quarter. When the time comes, it floats up with the water level. On both sides are two figures in golden armour, one holding a bell and the other holding a *cheng*. At night these gods sound the watch and strike the bell without the slightest inaccuracy. When the bell and the *cheng* are sounded, a lion on one side starts to dance and a phoenix on the other to flap its wings. On the east and west of the box is a temple of the sun and the moon. Six palace maidens stand in

ANCIENT GLORY   front of the temple. At noon and midnight, they come in pairs across the fairy
bridge and reach the temple of the Three Holy Ones and then return to their
place. Its ingenuity is beyond the imagination of men."

TABLE OF HISTORICAL EVENTS IN PEKING

Dynasty	Independent Dynasty	Adminis. Status	Name	Events
Yü B.C. 2255-2206			Yuchow	Four powerful families exiled beyond Nankow Pass.
Chou B.C. 1122-257		Prince of Yen	Chi, capital of Yen	Descendants of Yellow Emperor settled here in 12th century B. C. B. C. 723-222, Yen state. Around B. C. 300 powerful King of Yen built section of Great Wall.
Tsin B.C. 246-207		District	Shangku	About B. C. 214-210 Great Wall completed.
Han B.C. 206-220 A.D.		Prince of Yen	Yen, later Yuchow	Short-lived rebellions. A. D. 227 Prince of Yen taken by Wei.
Wei A.D. 220-264		Prince of Yen	Yuchow	Independent state ruling north-east China.
Chin 265-419		Prince of Fanyang etc.	Yuchow	From A.D. 307, North China under Hu tribes; many changes of regime.
North and South Dynasties 420-588				
Sui 589-618		District	Chochün	608, Grand Canal connected with Peking.
Tang 618-906		Military Governor	Yuchow, Fanyang etc.	757, short-lived rebellion of An Lushan, as "King of Yen." 760-910, 28 semi-independent Lu-lung military governors.
Five Dynasties 907-959				
North Sung 960-1126	Liao 907-1115 (Khitans)	Capital of Liao	Nanking; Yenching (from 1012)	Peking regarded as the "southern capital" of Liao since 937.
South Sung 1127-1279	Chin 1115-1234 (Nüchens)	Capital of Chin	Chungtu (1153)	1113-15, Chins took Peking from Liaos, gave it to Sung. 1115, Chin took over Peking. 1151, new Peking expanded.
Yuan 1280-1367 (Mongols)		Capital	Tatu (Kambaluk)	1215, Jenghiz Khan's army took Peking. 1260, Kublai Khan was crowned. 1264-7, Peking rebuilt on new site. 1275, Marco Polo first saw Kublai Khan. 1276, Mongols conquered Hang-chow, capital of South Sung.
Ming 1368-1643		Capital	Peiping; Peking after 1403	1368, Peking remodelled and extended. 1417-1420, extensive rebuilding under Yunglo. 1436, rebuilding continued. 1553-64, Outer Wall added.
Ching 1644-1910 (Manchus)		Capital	Peking	City unchanged, but beautified under Kangshi and Chienlung.

22. Street draughts-players: a typical Peking scene.

WARLORDS, DOWAGERS
AND CONCUBINES

IN WESTERN HISTORY, there have been many great queens, like Maria-Teresa of Austria or Elizabeth I of England. In China, such great queens are conspicuous by their absence, perhaps because good queens preferred to stay behind the throne and help their husbands with tact and wise counsel. But when Chinese queens broke through the wall of custom and tore open the beaded curtains behind which they were supposed to sit and whisper, heads flew fast. This happened with Lady Wu Tsehtien (reign: A. D. 684-704), who laid down a pattern long before the Imperial Capital was located at Peking. She wiped out the princes of her husband's royal house and tried to found a dynasty of her own.[15] An Lushan's rebellion (A. D. 755), which crippled if it did not destroy the Tang Imperial House, was started because Lady Yang Kweifei had adopted An Lushan, a man of her own age, as " godson." After giving the " baby " a bath on his anniversary she had his two hundred pounds wrapped up in sheets and carried across the court to the amusement and laughter of the courtiers.

Behind the façade of imperial rule we may often see the deeds of warlords, dowagers and concubines. Practically the whole of the Han and Ming Dynasties were plagued with the power of eunuchs, since eunuchs were closest to the queens and royal consorts. During the notorious periods of rule by eunuchs towards the end of the Ming Dynasty, the eunuchs could and did flog courtiers —to death if they so wished. This was unheard-of and unprecedented in Chinese history, since scholars of a certain degree had always been exempt from corporal punishment. While the officials were being flogged, stretchers were ready to carry them out, dead or alive. These half-men ruled through the power of the queens.

Chen Yuanyuan was a concubine, but she was not a bad woman. Nevertheless she played an important role in the collapse of the Ming Dynasty and in the Manchu conquest of China. When a rebel chief, Li Tsecheng, broke into the capital in 1643 and the last Ming emperor, Tsungcheng, hanged himself, Li captured the sweetheart of another general, Wu Sankwei. In order to recover his love, this Chen Yuanyuan, Wu asked the Manchus from across the Great Wall for help. The famous Manchu warrior Dorgun came in and drove out Li's ill-disciplined troops, but then refused to go back. Wu Sankwei had recovered the woman he loved, but now he realized his error. A Chinese at heart, he refused to submit to the Manchu conquerors, fled and established an independent kingdom on the southwest in Yunnan. For decades he resisted Manchu

23. The White Pagoda
at the Summer Palace.

24. A detail of
multiple roofs and tiling system.

65

overtures, living with Chen Yuanyuan as king and queen in a palace overlooking the great Kunming Lake, where he built her a pavilion with golden roofs.

Nearer our own time is the Dowager Empress Tsyshi, who has been written about profusely. She had great influence on the history of Peking, for she both built the Summer Palace, and contributed to bringing about the sack of the city in 1900. A contemporary of Queen Victoria, she dominated the political scene for half a century. Undoubtedly she had political sagacity, extraordinary strength of character, the gift of quick decision and an ability to hold the reins of government in tight hands. She had typical feminine intelligence where personal relationships were concerned. For palace intrigue she was superb, even in her young days when, as the young widow of Emperor Shienfeng (A. D. 1851-1861), her position was threatened. But she was nevertheless an ignorant, stubborn woman who held China back in the vital half-century when it was facing the western challenge, and when Japan, in a similar situation, transformed itself into a modern nation. Her mental background was astonishing. She was once heard to remark that she did not believe that a country like Portugal really existed. For Portugal was translated into Chinese as *Putaoya*, or " grape sprouts ".

"How could there really be a country called Grape Sprouts?" she asked.

Her rule culminated in the Boxer uprising, the siege of the Legations, their rescue, and finally the sack of Peking. The whole episode was almost incredible, like a tale from the Middle Ages. She accepted the advice of Yunglu, her lover, and of Prince Tuan, and believed in the magic of the Boxers. She ordered the siege and attack on the entire body of the foreign diplomatic corps! Yuan-Shih-kai had sounder common sense. As Governor of Shantung he did not believe in magic and he drove the Boxers out of his province; nor did the educated Chinese governors, like Chang Chih-tung, believe in the Boxers. Yuan had a simple way of dealing with the fantastic claims of the Boxers that their incantations made them bullet proof. He asked for a demonstration. Ten Boxers were called in. His advisers who believed in the Boxers were standing by. He ordered one of his captains to shoot. Marvellous to behold, the shots left the Boxers unharmed. His advisers were elated. Then Yuan himself pulled out a revolver and pumped bullets into the Boxers one by one. He had planned with his captain to shoot from an unloaded pistol.

Here is the picture of the tragedy as I have tried to sum it up in *Moment in Peking*.

" The Empress Dowager had hesitated between avoiding a war with the foreign powers and using the Boxers, a strange, unknown, frightening force whose one object was to destroy the foreigners in China and who claimed magic protection against foreign bullets. The Court issued orders one day for arrest of the Boxer leaders, and the next day appointed the pro-Boxer Prince Tuan as minister for foreign affairs. Court intrigue played an important part in this reversal of the decision to suppress the Boxers. The Empress Dowager had already deprived her nephew the Emperor of his actual power, and was planning to depose him. She favoured Prince Tuan's son, a worthless rascal, as successor to the throne. Thinking that a foreign war would increase his personal power and obtain the throne for his son, Prince Tuan encouraged the Empress Dowager to believe that the Boxers' magic actually made them proof against the foreign bullets. Besides, the Boxers had threatened to capture ' one Dragon and two Tigers ' to sacrifice to heaven for betrayal of their nation, the ' Dragon ' being the reformist Emperor whose ' hundred days of reform ' two years earlier had shocked the conservative mandarinate, and the ' Tigers ' being the elderly Prince Ching and Li Hungchang, who had been in charge of the foreign policy.

" Prince Tuan forged a joint note from the diplomatic corps of Peking asking

25. Interior of the Temple of Confucius, showing a hanging bell, stele and stone drums.

66

the Empress Dowager to restore the Emperor to actual power, thus making the old woman believe that the foreign powers stood in the way of her plan to depose the Emperor, so that she decided to throw in her lot with the Boxers, whose secret of power was their war cry of 'driving out the Oceanic People.' Some enlightened cabinet ministers had opposed the Boxers on account of the burning of the European Legations, advocated by the Boxers, which was against Western usage; but these opponents had been killed by the power of Prince Tuan. The Chancellor of the Peking University had committed hara-kiri by disembowelling himself.

"The Boxers were actually within the capital. A lieutenant-colonel who had been sent out to fight them had been ambushed and killed, and his soldiers had joined the Boxers. Highly popular and triumphant, the Boxers had captured Peking, killing foreigners and Christian Chinese and burning their churches. The diplomatic corps protested, but Kang Yi, sent to investigate the Boxers, reported that they were 'sent from Heaven to drive out the Oceanic People and wipe out China's shame' and secretly let tens of thousands of them into the capital.

"Once inside, the Boxers, under the covert protection of the Empress Dowager and Prince Tuan, terrorized the city. They roamed the streets, hunting and killing 'First Hairies' and 'Second and Third Hairies.' The 'First Hairies' were the foreigners; the 'Second and Third Hairies' were the Christians, clerks in foreign firms, and any other English-speaking Chinese. They went about burning churches and foreign houses, destroying foreign mirrors, foreign umbrellas, foreign clocks and foreign paintings. Actually they killed more Chinese than foreigners. Their method of proving a Chinese to be a 'Second Hairy' was simple. Suspects were made to kneel before a Boxer altar in the open street, while a piece of paper containing a message to their patron god was burned, and the suspect was pronounced guilty or not guilty according to whether the ashes flew up or flew down. Altars would be set up in the streets toward sunset, and the people who showed obedience to the Boxers would burn incense while they danced their monkey dance, the Monkey Spirit being one of the most popular of their patron gods. The smell of incense filled the streets, and one could believe oneself living in the magic land of *Hsiyuchi* once more. Even important officials had set up altars and invited the Boxer leaders to their homes, and servants had joined the Boxers to tyrannize over their masters.

"...The foreign shop Powei was looted. They smashed all the watches, clocks and glasses. Someone took a bottle of foreign perfume and drank it for foreign wine. He turned white and fell on the floor and shouted that he had been poisoned by foreign concoctions. A boy working in the firm said they smashed the electric talking machine (telephone) and cut the wire because they thought it was a devilish land-mine to blow them up. Someone caught up a foreign mannequin, tore off the dress, and carried the naked foreign woman across the street. The crowd cheered and had the greatest fun out of that lady. Children ran and scrambled for her golden hair and started to fight among themselves..."

For those who wish to read about this story, there is no better book than *China Under the Empress Dowager* by Bland and Backhouse. Putnam Weale also gives a long first hand account of the sack of Peking, in *Indiscreet Letters from Peking* (1906).

The tottering Manchu empire, really old because it was incapable of learning, lingered on. The stubborn, ignorant woman had completed the corruption from within, having learned nothing and forgotten nothing, even from the disastrous fall of Peking and her personal flight to Si-an in the northwest. She returned in 1902, stubborn and uncontrite of heart, and again shut up the Emperor in the South Sea Palace. The Chinese demand for constitutional monarchy went on for another ten years until their patience was exhausted. Then, in 1908, she

26. Part of a city wall with camel-train.

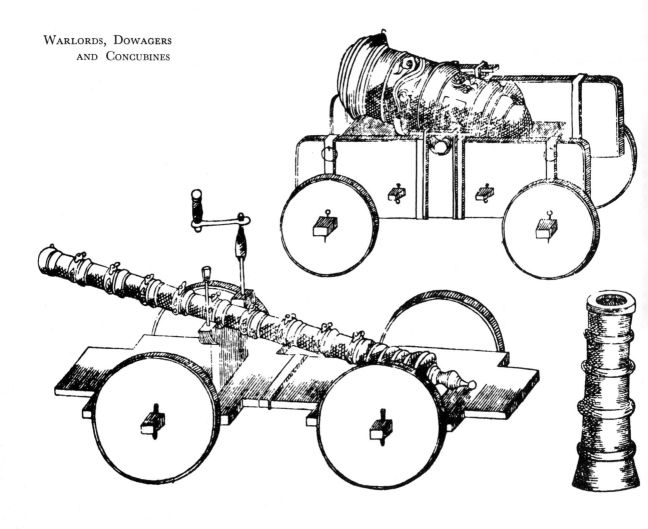

died. But the demoralized regime could not pull itself together. Sun Yatsen, the republican, won, not because the Chinese thought a republic better than a constitutional monarchy, but because they hated the Manchus. The Chinese Republic was established in 1911.

The first stage of the history of the republic was dominated no longer by Dowagers or concubines, but by warlords. The rule of the warlords after the collapse of the empire provided a most amazing and colourful spectacle. Typical figures were Chang Tsolin, the Manchurian warlord; the "Dog-Meat General" Chang Tsungchang who drove the liberal professors of Peking University out of Peking; President Tsao Kun who made his favourite pedicurist sit above a premier at public dinners. The "Dog-Meat General" used to receive foreign consuls with a White Russian mistress sitting on his lap. He loved the Russian girl and the Russian girl loved a poodle, and he made a whole regiment pass in review before the poodle.

He loved his country profoundly and was intensely loyal to his mother. He played fair; if he took another man's wife, he gave the husband a nice job as police commissioner of a city...

27

29 28

30

31

32

33

34

35 36

Does human nature ever change? The loves and sufferings and the timeless patience of the Peking populace never change. The trappings do. A French journalist published a story in *Figaro* in 1956 that when he was staying at a hotel in Peking to attend a kind of international conference, he was woken one night at one a.m. by the loud sound of megaphones and gongs, calling all residents of Peking to get up and kill the sparrows. Sparrows, it is understood, are like human beings: prevent them from sleep for a few nights and they are psychologically conditioned to give up the struggle for existence. This was done on a national scale. Sparrows eat grain and are an enemy to socialist production and reconstruction. They must be ruthlessly exterminated. It is scientifically calculated that sparrows cannot keep on the wing for more than a couple of hours. After a period of noise and fright when they were unable to take rest in trees, they fell down dead and were exterminated. The poor sparrows...

So passed the glory that was Mongol and the power that was Manchu. An extravagant Chinese queen once sent the peasants to kill the frogs in the country around her palace because they disturbed her sleep at night. The irrefutable fact remains that the frogs survived; they had nature on their side. I am quite sure that the innocent sparrows will some day chirp merrily once more in the farmayards and in the hutungs of Peking, as of old.

WARLORDS, DOWAGERS AND CONCUBINES

34. The Five Pagoda Temple, in the western suburb.

35. 36. Lamaistic rock sculptures at Jade Fountain Hill.

Contest in archery for military officers

37. 'Horses and Groom':
painting by Han Kan
(Tang Dynasty).

37

THE PALACES AND PLEASANCES

IT IS ART WHICH has made Peking into a jewel city, a city with shining, golden roofs; it is art which has planned the long avenues and high gate towers, and enriched the charm of living. Not only architecture, but the arts of painting, sculpture, ceramics, antiques and old books printed from woodblocks — those within the Palace Museum and those found in Liulichang—all these have made Peking what it is. The Palace Museum contains all the priceless accumulations of centuries, kept within the royal palaces and rarely seen by the eyes of man. It used to be housed in Wenhuatien and Wuyingtien on the right and left of the central palace, the Taihotien. In 1933, the treasures were removed to Nanking, for the signs of a coming Japanese war were already all too evident. From Nanking, these treasures were again moved with the utmost care to Formosa and stored in the vaults of Taichung. The best of Chinese art is all there. It still bears the name of Kukung Powuyuan, or Museum of the Ancient Palaces, and people still associate these treasures in their minds with Peking, as we associate the treasures of the Louvre with Paris.

Certain characteristics of Chinese architecture — those of form, line, colour and composition — are basic in conception, and dictate the differences from western architecture. The use of colour is much less evident in western palatial structures, such as Versailles or Hampton Court, and for that matter in all the ancient castles of England and France. The predominant colour of European palaces, like Versailles, seems to be a prevailing white or a time-honoured buff and grey. This can be extremely beautiful, provided it is set against green parkland and surrounded with trees. The Peking palaces on the other hand, and their subsidiary structures, were designed with colour very much in the architect's mind. This was made possible through the use of glazed tiles, or *liuli wa*, obtaining shades of enamel red, yellow, blue, green, lavender or turquoise, and through reliance on paint and lacquer on woodwork.

The neglect of stone as building material places limits on Chinese architecture. Cost of labour certainly could not have been a factor with the tyrants. The result of using poor materials is that decay is swift, and for all the millenniums of imperial splendour China has today relatively little to show in the way of ancient architectural monuments. Where stone has been used, it has survived for centuries, for example in carvings on cliffs and engravings on tombs. This is strikingly brought home when one visits the old Summer Palace, which was destroyed as late as 1860 in the war between the Manchu emperors and the

38. 'Partridge and Sparrow attributed to Huang Chutsai (Five Dynasties).

79

British and French. Of all that vast imperial pleasance with terraces and pavilions and towers, truly the greatest pleasure garden of the world, the only thing that remains today are the " Italian Ruins " or remains of the Italian Palace, built of stone by French and Italian rococo architects. Rococo pillars lie about, and the friezes and pediments are strewn among the growing grass. They are stone and therefore remain as ruins. All the rest of that fabulous pleasure ground of the Emperors Kangshi and Chienlung which made a western castle seem like a toy in size has disappeared. Only ponds and reeds remain.

This is true also of the great Tsin, Han and Tang palaces, all situated about Si-an. Standing on top of the renowned Opangkung of the first emperor of Tsin (third century B. C.), I saw it was only a terraced mud mound today, some fifty or sixty feet high and a hundred yards long, rather resembling a runway for airplanes. The magnificent Nightless Palace (Weiyangkun) of the great Han Wuti (second century B. C.) is today, as far as appearances are concerned, only a tall mound of mud standing in the northwest of the city. The race-course and jewelled towers of the famous Queen Yang Kweifei (eighth century A. D.) in the northern outskirts of modern Si-an are replaced by wheatfields and farmhouses. All the ancient buildings in Peking have entirely vanished—for example the twelfth century Chin palaces. The ancient Mongol city walls made of mud now appear as a series of broken mud ramparts slowly yielding to the ravages of time.

When I saw the throne room in Peking, what struck me most was the dilapidated conditions of the throne dais and the throne itself, made of wood, and not very good wood at that, covered with cracked and faded paint. Of course the theory was that if fresh paint was applied every year it could look like new in vermilion and gold and green. But the idea of permanence was ruled out.

The whole idea of a palace in China is different from that of the west. The Chinese palaces are never like an army regiment in a straight closed formation, but rather like one deployed and marching in separate platoons. European palaces usually consist of a huge structure, with a front garden like the Tuileries before the Louvre. They contain endless rooms connected by a covered corridor going all around so that one seldom has to go through a large and extensive courtyard in the open into another building. This is true even of the Versailles Palace, even though the gardens are immense. A palace is, in other words, one building. The Peking palaces, on the other hand, following the idea of separate courts as in domestic architecture, set up different structures in separate courts, connected by long pavements or sheltered corridors. They are divided into separate living units. Hence comes the concentration on open spaces in the great ceremonial halls, with increasing emphasis on the approaches of terraced marble steps and balustrades and long vistas in between.

The palaces are strictly confined within the Forbidden City, with high, crenellated pink walls and look-out towers. It rather resembles a fortified city, with great towers standing on heavy walls, some thirty or forty feet high and fifty feet wide at the foundation. Enclosing the Forbidden City is the Huangcheng, or Imperial City, also enclosed in a lower pink wall, but not having the same fortified appearance. The area which lies between the walls of the Imperial City and the Forbidden City is all taken up by the Sea Palaces on the west, and on the east by various official buildings that had to do with the administration and supplies of the palace household.

The southern end of the Forbidden City is occupied by the three great ceremonial halls, the Taihotien, the Chunghotien and the Paohotien, called in Chinese the " Three Great Palaces." The Taihotien may be called the Throne Hall, the place for great ceremonial occasions like the coronation, and public

40 41
42 43

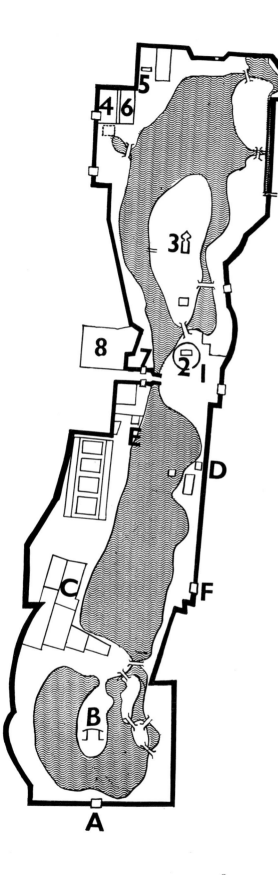

PEIHAI, CHUNGHAI AND NANHAI

PEIHAI

1 Round City
2 Alabaster Buddha
3 White Dagoba
4 Great Western Paradise
5 Nine Dragon screen
6 Sungpo Library
7 Jade Rainbow Bridge
8 National Library

CHUNGHAI AND NANHAI

A Shinhuamen
B Ingtai (where Emperor Kwangshü was imprisoned for ten years)
C Yuan Shih-kai's Presidential Palace
D Temple of Great Mercy
E Tsykwangko
F East entrance

40. Pailou at the Hall of Classics, Imperial College – North Peking.

41. *Huapiao*, or decorative pillar, at Ming tombs.

42. Stone arch at the entrance to the tomb of Emperor Yungcheng (r. 1723-1735) at Hsiling, a group of tombs of Manchu Emperors, west of Peking.

43. A *paifang*, or decorative archway.

receptions on imperial birthdays and on New Year's Day, when vassals were received. The middle one is less important, a convenient resting-place chiefly, where the emperor could take his leisure before coming out to the front hall. The Paohotien is mainly remembered as the place where the emperor received those scholars who had succeeded in the imperial examinations. The real audience hall is at Chienchingkung, at the back of the last hall and inside the imperial residences, which may be called the Inner Court, or the Winter Palace, a group of buildings and courts for the emperors, their princes, and empresses.[16]

Architecture may be divided into two broad classes, formal and informal, the former aiming at splendour and elegance, the latter at privacy, irregularity, surprise and contrast, the requirements of a peaceful and beautiful residence. The latter class applies to residential quarters and house gardens. The distinction is somewhat similar to that between the formal writing of declarations, dedication speeches and historic documents on the one hand and the informal essay on the other hand, where the personal point of view and warmth and intimate revelations constitute the chief charms. The Taihotien is representative of the formal, impressive public structures, and the Sea Palaces are representative of the imperial pleasure grounds. Certain characteristics of Chinese architecture stand out in each.

In the ceremonial halls in the southern end of the Forbidden City, the first impression is that of serenity. This is the word I have chosen to describe the architectural effect; it contrasts with the soul-uplifting and skyward aspirations of the Gothic cathedral. In both cases, the effect of grandeur is achieved by majestic proportions. To one used to seeing Chartres and other cathedrals in France, the sheer bulk of the Cathedral at Burgos and the huge Gothic columns of the Cathedral at Seville can still be breathtaking. In the case of Peking, the magnificence of the palaces is suggested first by the half-mile-long approach from Chienmen to Tienanmen. The Tienanmen rises seventy or eighty feet high with a complete tower above, like a fortified wall, and the gate which penetrates the wall is at least seventy or eighty feet deep. On the outside the large square easily accommodates a hundred thousand people. This is the limit of the Imperial City, and on the inside one has yet to pass through two extensive courts, through the Tuanmen and then Wumen, which marks the beginning of the Forbidden City. The Forbidden City has the charm of sanctity and mystery; like the apple of Eden, what is forbidden sounds tempting and good. The Wumen is also fortified with high towers on top of the wall, and beyond it one enters the enormous court of the Taihotien. Only on formal occasions when the emperor came out, as for worship at the Temple of Heaven, or on victorious return from a campaign, were these central gates open. Entrances are provided on the sides, the Tunghuamen and Shihuamen, for the courtiers to enter the palace grounds.

Now the whole idea of the majestic approach becomes apparent. This court of the Taihotien is vast, about two hundred yards long and the same in width. The open space in front is part of the imperial grandeur. The architects of Yunglo had carefully calculated the effect to be achieved, for buildings of this kind can be appreciated only at a proper distance. The enormous pavement, the five marble bridges over the Golden Water Stream before the Taihomen, the triple marble terraces leading up to the Taihotien, and the low and sweeping golden roofs of the hall itself form a unity, one architectural concept. The hall stands on a raised stone foundation, reached by flights of steps across the white marble balustrade, giving one the proper feeling of ascent to a sacred precinct. On both sides of the yard run covered corridors. The flights of steps are divided into three sections, the middle one in the form of a slab of stone engraved with dragons

44. 'A Palace Concert':
school of Chou Wen-chu;
(Tang Dynasty)
hanging scroll, ink and
colours on silk,
$19^1/_8'' \times 27^3/_8''$.

84

44

and other symbols, used only by the emperor when he was carried in his sedan chair. On the terrace above these steps before the hall, is a large stone pavement with a marble sundial, a marble bushel and a bronze crane and tortoise, symbols of long life, and other large iron pots for keeping water in case of fire.

The Taihotien is 110 feet high, 200 feet wide and 100 feet deep, a measurement which roughly equals the audience hall of Kublai Khan. The hall is now empty. In the centre stands the throne dais, some thirty feet square, mounted by steps on three sides. Up above, the ceiling is painted in squares of green and gold. Over the throne dais stands a board with four characters in gold, *Chengta Kwangming*, emphasizing the idea of rectitude and openness of mind, with nothing to hide. (To translate the word *kwangming* here by " brilliance " would be incorrect.) I have already remarked on the dilapidated condition of the throne dais, whose appearance chiefly depended on the use of lacquer. But it does not need much imagination to picture the magnificence of the scene, when the emperor sat in court surrounded by palace guards and courtiers. It is well conveyed in the woodcuts in the Japanese book, *Tangtu Mingsheng Tukwei*, representing the scene outside the Wumen and the entertainment of vassals at the Taihotien.

An interesting feature, revealed in these woodcuts and corroborated by Chinese records, is that pairs of elephants stood opposite each other across the gateway. When the courtiers had passed, the elephants came together and locked their trunks to block the central path outside the Wumen. The elephants were kept in the Elephant House inside Shunchymen. Just behind is the smaller Chunghotien, where one day in 1898 Emperor Kwangshü was arrested by his aunt, as he was preparing to come out and give audience.

The serenity of the palace buildings is brought about by the sweeping rather than aspiring roofs. Juliet Bredon has rightly remarked that there is not a straight line in the whole roof; " even the main sweep of the tiles has a slight curve, a ripple, which is not accidental but expressly introduced to charm the eye without detracting from the purity of line or its restful simplicity." [17] Similarly in the Acropolis the columns were not perfectly vertical. They were inclined inward but so slightly that the bend was almost invisible. Much has been made of a theory about the Chinese curved roofs taking their origin from the natural lines of the Mongolian tent. The argument seems plausible on the surface. Yet it is entirely artificial, for it pays no attention to the Chinese instinct for form and line.

As one stands marvelling at the perfection and purity of line of these palaces and the Temple of Heaven, one is bound to feel that instinctive sense of form and composition, that subtle appreciation of proportion, of structural support and ancillary curves which comes directly from the aesthetic training in Chinese calligraphy.

One of the basic tenets of calligraphy is the *interplay of rigid straight lines and curving forms*. Obviously the curving roofs which generally occupy half the height of a building, form a harmonious whole with the straight base or pillars below. Curves without a solid framework produce an effect of grace without strength, while straight lines throughout result in dead rigidity. We have an example of this in the United Nations building in New York and the impression is one of strength without grace. The building has the clean cut lines of a foot rule, that is about all. Only by the interplay of straight lines and curves can a juxtaposition of lines be brought into harmonious unity. Thus both strength and grace are necessary to anything of beauty, whether in architecture or in the human form or character.

In the Peking palaces, the roofs become the most distinctive part of the structure, on which the whole line of the building depends. The use of glazed tiles,

45. Lady Kuo-kuo and her sisters setting forth on an outing': a twelfth-century copy, attributed to Li Kung-lin, of an eighth-century scroll, after Chang Hsuan; ink and colours on silk, height 13¼".

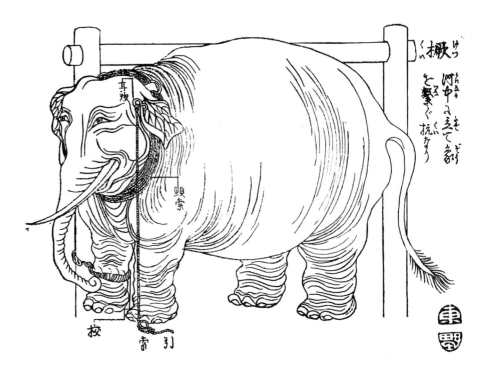

Washing elephants and the
instruments used

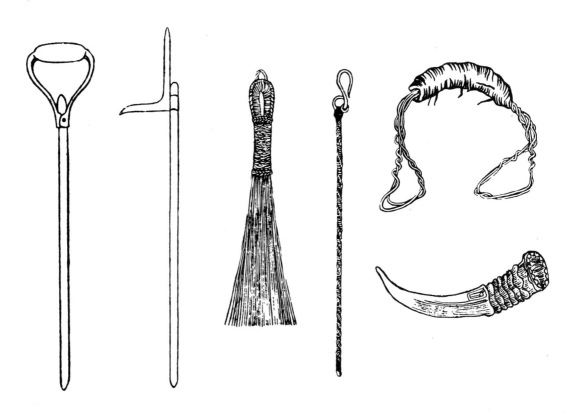

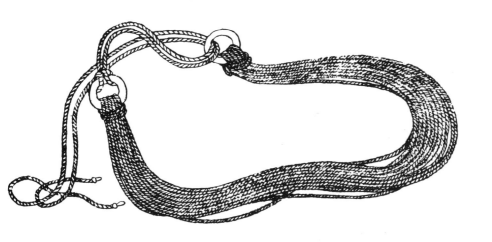

89

admitting the use of colour, again shifts the emphasis to the roofs. Consequently, as will be seen in any colour reproductions of the palace grounds, the intricate development of simple or multiple overlapping roofs (seen also in Japanese temples and palaces) constitutes almost the most decorative part of the building.

Ancestor worship always played a large role in Chinese society, so special importance attaches to the Ancestral Temple of the Imperial House at the southeastern corner of the Imperial City. Here on the first day of every quarter of the year offerings of bullock and lamb were made to the spirits of the past emperors of the house. Here, according to the ancient custom of *kaomiao*, announcements were made to the deceased spirits when some great decision affecting the fortunes of the house had been decided upon. A peculiar feature of the imperial Taimiao, not found in the ancestral temples of the common people, is that the hall is arranged in compartments, each of which is devoted to one emperor. Throne seats are provided for each emperor and his consorts, the emperor's seat in the centre and those of his consorts on the sides. Thus Kangshi had four consorts and four such seats are provided; Chienlung had two, Shienfeng had three, and poor Kwangshü had only one. The yard is covered with old cypresses where a great many crows gather. The birds always know by experience that in such a neighbourhood shooting is forbidden, and this is true of many such sacred grounds in other parts of China.

For me however, the most impressive sight was the Imperial Library at the Wenyuanko, at the back of the Wenhuatien. It is a two-storied building, where the books are kept in casings of silk or brocade, fastened with jade pins on the side. There were special studies for the emperor, both on the ground and the top floors, where he could do his reading. The house contains one of the four handwritten sets of the great library of Emperor Chienlung, the famous *Syku Chuanshu*. One of the sets at the Yuanmingyuan was set on fire by the victorious Allied troops in 1860, a time when there was a complete lack of understanding of China among Europeans. The European soldiers had no inkling of what a treasure they were burning. Emperor Chienlung had given orders for a nation-wide search for valuable old books. The books were forwarded to the capital, and an academy of editors set to work to examine them and compare them with other known editions. A list was made of those selected and they were copied by hand for inclusion in this great collection. A supplementary list was given of works which were of merit but not so included. The editors were erudite scholars, particularly the old scholar Chi Shiaolan, a man of great wit, humour and sterling scholarship, of whom Chienlung was very fond. To this day the brief editorial comments in the *Tiyao* on the style, origin and value of each book in the Syku Library remain classics of their kind. Like the great earlier collection of Yunglo, the *Yunglo Tatien*, which, except for some 200 extant volumes, has also been burned and lost to posterity, this collection was carefully lettered by trained scholars, and every brush stroke scrutinized. The ink was excellent, the paper white and heavy and of the best *shüan* quality, and the volumes were bound in silk.

Much of the early Chinese resentment against the Manchu conquerors evaporated when the Chinese saw the great love of Chinese learning in both Kangshi and Chienlung. These were the great patrons of art and literature, and impressive encyclopedias, dictionaries and reference books were compiled by their orders. Fortunately, also, both Kangshi and Chienlung enjoyed reigns of sixty years. In fact, when Chienlung reached the sixty-first year of his reign, he retired, saying that he did not dare exceed the great Kangshi in the length of his reign. He lived on in peace and comfort at the eastern side of the Winter Palace for a few years more before he died. Chienlung had so identified himself with Chinese

46. Pavilion on a bridge
at the Summer Palace.

46

culture and wrote such competent poetry and calligraphy that there was a persist-
ent report, which may not be more than gossip, that he was born of Chinese
parents and put on the throne only by a ruse when as an infant he was smuggled
into the palace.

The last Manchu emperor was placed on the throne when he was four years
old. When I was in Peking, Puyi was a young man of twenty, still living within
the Winter Palace, studying English under Sir R. F. Johnston, from whom he
got the wonderful royal name of Henry. A friend of mine saw this " Henry Puyi " with a can of Huntley & Palmer's biscuits on his table, no doubt introduced
by his English tutor. He was also seen to tear off pages of old editions to wipe his
nose with. Through no fault of his own, he was driven out of the palace by the
melodramatic " Christian " general Feng Yushiang, kidnapped by the Japanese,
taken to Tientsin, then installed as Emperor of the puppet Manchukuo, then taken
by the Russians when they marched into Manchuria after the Hiroshima bomb.

The last we heard of him was in 1960, when he was working somewhere as a
factory hand around Mukden. He had made a clean breast of the " bourgeois "
sins in his blood and pledged his heart to work for the successful completion of
the socialist reconstruction.

Of the Sea Palaces, Nanhai, Chunghai and Peihai simply mean the South,
Middle and North Seas. Here are the pleasure grounds of the emperors,
covered with old trees and dominated by the Tibetan-looking dagoba in Peihai,
visible from a great distance. The French call this queer-shaped structure the
bouteille de peppermint, which indeed it resembles. Here stood the centre of Kublai
Khan's former palaces, their halls hung with wildcat and ermine and their floors
covered with black sable. Kublai Khan's falcon house was on the west; Marco
Polo informs us that his park was filled with his " white stags and fallow deer,
gazelles and roebucks and fine squirrels of various sorts "; and Odoric was excited
by the technical wonders of mechanical peacocks. There was also a water clock
made of gold (see Chapter 4).

On the South side lies the Nanhai, a scene of exquisite beauty and also of
pathetic tragedy. On a small island joined to the land on the north by a thin
strip is the Ingtai, usually inadequately translated as " Ocean Terrace." Actually
Ing is meant to recall the fairy islands reputed to exist in the China Sea. Here
the reformist emperor Kwangshü was imprisoned for a total of about ten
years. The story recalls that of the prince in an iron mask thrown into a dungeon
on an island off Cannes who rotted there and died unknown to the world.
Kwangshü's fate is not quite as tragic as that. The island, though extremely small,
is beautiful, and Kwangshü was at liberty within the confines of the small island
studded with beautiful structures. But he lived under the sharp surveillance of
the eunuchs who knew their lives depended upon obedience to the Empress
Dowager. The eunuchs were changed frequently so that no one could enter into a
conspiracy for his escape. Once a eunuch in the chilly winter saw holes in the
paper windows and, taking pity on the young emperor, had the window re-
papered. The eunuch was dismissed the next day, for nothing happened at Ingtai
which Kwangshü's aunt, the imperious old dowager, did not immediately hear
about. He wanted to put the Chinese government through a series of modern
reforms, but his plans were foiled by the treachery of Yuan Shih-kai. In his thirties,
he must have developed an attitude of rueful resignation and contented himself
with admiring the changing seasons in the Nanhai lake. It was not so bad, for
what could a gentleman do against such a tigress of an aunt? His favourite consort
had been thrown into a well on the empress's direct orders the night before she
and the emperor fled before the Allied soldiers into remote Shensi during the
Boxer uprising in 1900.

47. 'Listening
to the Wind in the Pines ':
Ma Lin, dated 1246,
in Southern Sung Court style;
hanging scroll,
ink and colours on silk
width 43 1/2".

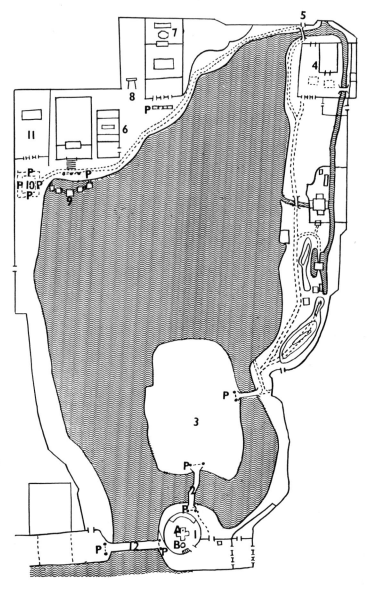

PEIHAI

 1   Round City
 A   Alabaster Buddha
 B   Jade Jar
 2   Centipede Bridge
 3   Chiunghuatao (Emerald Isle)
 4   Hall of Sericulture
 5   North Entrance
 6   Sungpo Library
 7   Ten Buddhas, Little Western Paradise
 8   Nine Dragon Screen
 9   Wulungting (Five Pavilion Bridge)
10   Hall of Goddess of Mercy
11   Great Western Paradise
12   Jade Rainbow Bridge (Yuhungchiao)
PPP Pailous

48. Stone boat
at the Summer Palace.

The story of "Pearl Consort's Well," as told by a eunuch who was an eye-witness, is that the Empress, after personally giving the order, sat in the opposite court to see it carried out. Her malice sprang out of the sense of being endangered. Disaster had come about because of her policy of encouraging the Boxers. The emperor himself had nothing to do with this. But Chenfei, or Pearl Consort, always had a mind of her own. At the last moment, she tried to convince the empress dowager that the emperor should stay behind to negotiate with the foreign conquerors, as it was well known that he was sympathetic to "the foreign devils." The old woman feared that the foreign troops by this sudden turn of events could have brought the emperor back to power. This she could not possibly tolerate. The emperor was ordered to go with her. Besides, Chenfei had always had too much spirit and intelligence, and one woman of intelligence in the palace was enough. Today the spot just inside the northeast gate at the back of the Inner Palace is always pointed out to tourists as the Chenfeiching, or "Pearl Consort's Well."

48

History is always full of "great" queens and empresses. The Tang empress, Wu Tsehtien, proposed to have the emperor, her own son, in whose name she was ruling, tried for treason to herself. He had for years been held *incommunic-ado* with the outside world and was forbidden to see visitors. It took an ordinary honest palace manservant to slit his own stomach and pull out his intestines in protest on behalf of the young emperor and stop the empress's injustice to her own son.

The case of Kwangshü needed to be told because of the senseless eulogy I read in English about this "great" woman ruler, master of palace intrigue, but also because it influenced the whole course of modern Chinese history. It could hardly have been a pure coincidence that the emperor should die just one day before his aunt in 1908. The plain fact was that the thought of the emperor surviving her and perhaps taking revenge upon her sacred memory was intolerable to the old woman, who knew that her days were numbered. So the emperor conveniently died one day before her. The story is told that the emperor bit his finger and wrote with blood his last wish that Yuan Shih-kai, who so treacherously betrayed him in 1898, should be banished forever from the court. Whether the story is true or not, Yuan was banished from office during the four years after Kwangshü's death, until he rose to power again during the 1911 revolution.

The South, Middle and North Seas witnessed profound tragedy in a series of events which connect up like a chain. At the south end Emperor Kwangshü died a prisoner, betrayed by a man associated with the Middle Sea, Yuan Shih-kai. Yuan came into power again after the founding of the Republic because he controlled the army, and in 1915 he prepared to make himself emperor. His plans were upset by a man called Tsai Sungpo, who raised a rebellion against him in Yunnan in 1916. The name of Tsai Sungpo has been perpetuated by the library situated at the northwest corner of the North Sea. In the face of the rebellion Yuan's contemplated monarchy collapsed like a house of cards because public sentiment was against a monarchy. To be at such a pinnacle of power was to be isolated from the public, and Yuan was methodically deceived by the conspirators, who wanted him to believe that the whole nation approved of the monarchist plot. Liang Shihyi (nicknamed the "God of Wealth") according to current stories, had a newspaper plant set up. Each morning he presented Yuan with newspapers from Shanghai. Keeping the news items, he had the editorial changed and printed in Peking, from which Yuan formed the impression that public opinion was clamouring for the restoration of a Chinese monarchy. Some dying words of the last Ming emperor sounded very much like the last thoughts of Yuan Shih-kai: "My ministers have deceived me."

Since the Republic was founded in 1911, most of the area of the Three Seas has been thrown open to the public. Near the head of the Jade Rainbow Bridge, separating the Middle from the North Sea, stands the Peking National Library, a building in fine taste and in harmony with the classical style of the surroundings. This area, particularly the Chunghai, or Middle Sea, was the favourite haunt of the Empress Dowager. Boys and girls can now go boating or skating on the lakes. In the days of the empire, it was strictly forbidden ground. Here at the Tsykwangtien, Emperor Tungchy (A. D. 1862-1877) held his first audience with the foreign diplomats. Forty or fifty feet high, the building was not so impressive as the big ceremonial halls, but it was more intimate. The place is studded with architectural gems, here a glimpse of a curved roof hidden among trees, there a decorative archway guards the approach to a bridge, here a screen of glazed and coloured tiles, there a giant Buddha; but the whole is discreet and in harmony with the landscape. An exception is a hideous European-style building, started by the Empress Dowager, as a mere whim, made more ugly by Yuan

49. 'The White Eagle';
Sung, embroidery on cut silk.

97

竹坨先生之像

Chu Yi-chun, author of the *Jyshia Chiuwen Tsao*

Shih-kai when he renovated it to serve as his presidential palace. Against its typically oriental surroundings, it stands out like an eyesore to every western tourist.

Juliet Bredon has written beautifully about the indefinable beauty of the three Seas area. " To analyse the charm of this forgotten corner of Peihai.... is impossible. It is a savour that must be tasted, a perfume inhaled, a colour seen with our own eyes. It is in the reflection of willows in the lake. It is in the gray stone embankments writhing like dragons along the shores. It is in the flight of ducks towards the south. It is in the flowing weeds creeping to caress the broken marble balustrades and the tender shrubs pushing their way through a yellow roof. It is in the shadows of the tiles on blue waters, and the purple tints of crows' wings on mauve gateways. It is in the solitary heron standing in the sunset on a rock, motionless as a bronze figure upon his pedestal. It is in the remembrance of the past staring at us wistfully, and the desolation of the present softly veiled by the golden dust."

50. ' Feeding Horses in a Moonlit Garden ': Jen Jen-fa, fourteenth century; ink and colours on silk.

Juliet Bredon, niece of Sir Robert Hart who organised the Chinese postal system, writes about Peking with great feeling and sometimes with great beauty. Her book, *Peking*, is justly famous as the standard book in English on this ancient

避人出鳥不成啼

集墨蹊蹊有古
風夏家之法按
吟中神情自
是清雨逸骨格
雖饒秀且雄僧
寺幾區心與淨
空帆千里畫難
寶湧煙割截失
名氏慘淡經營
孰解同
丁亥仲夏月
漸老

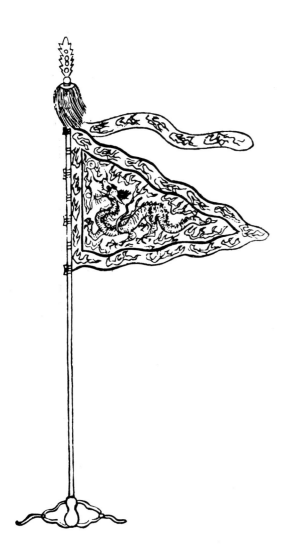

capital. All the temples and spots she writes about are invested with the feelings
of her personal visits. It is a strange coincidence that the names of the best
writers about Peking start with the letter "B." Bretschneider has contributed the
best archæological research. Bredon writes about all the forgotten corners with
the intelligent sympathy of one searching for what has been lost. J. P. O. Bland
and Backhouse, working as a pair, combining the Chinese scholarship of Backhouse with the vivid pen of Bland, have produced two historical books which read
like detective novels, in *The Annals and Memoirs of the Court of Peking* and *China
under the Empress Dowager*. With no intention of decrying the contributions of
other writers, the value of the four books mentioned above will always remain.

The marble curved bridge separating the Chunghai from the Peihai is called
the Jade Rainbow Bridge. It has always been a public thoroughfare, for this is
the point where people could cross from the city into the Imperial City. On
both sides one gets glimpses of the lakes. At the eastern end is the famous Tuancheng, connecting it with the island of the great white dagoba, known as Paita.
The Tuancheng or Round City is small, but it contains the alabaster Buddha
with a Mona Lisa smile, a work of supreme beauty and perfection. [18] It is said
that no matter how white a piece of jade may be, it pales in lustre if held close
to this alabaster Buddha. The figure is placed behind a glass which, however,

51. 'Walking on
Mountain Path in Spring':
Ma Yuan, joint founder of
the Ma-Hsia School
of Sung court painting.

52. 'River Landscape':
Hsia Kuei;
ink on paper.

enables the visitor to look at it from fairly close. In the yard is another rare object, the jade jar, some two feet high, on which are carved dragons and fish. It could quite well have been a relic from Kublai Khan, one of those jade vessels which Marco Polo described as worth the ransom of four towns put together—a pearl-tasselled jade vessel, standing " two paces in height." Of course there are similar jade jars, like that in Chienlung's room at Yangshingtien in the Inner Palace, but the size of this example is exceptional. According to Chinese records, this jar was lost when the Mongol House fell. Chienlung discovered it in a small temple, paid $1,000 for it and had it removed and placed here. He inscribed it with a poem by himself. It is well to remember that we are standing here right on the island which saw the glory of the Mongol, and before that the Chin rulers.

The white dagoba is of a very extraordinary and un-Chinese form and students in the park could look across the lotus-filled lake at its white reflection in the water. Its tremendous size is not appreciated until one approaches close to it and mounts the terrace which forms its base. It is probably the highest point in the whole of Peking City. The form of a dagoba is usually a thick, rounded dome, with a tiny structure on top, and is reminiscent of Buddhist reliquaries found in the region of Tibet, Siam and Burma. That it occupies such a prominent position at the Peihai Palace shows the depth of Buddhist influence since the twelfth century. In fact, Buddhist influence began as early as the fourth, fifth and sixth centuries (witness the sculptures at Yunkang, in the next province). The Chinese have accepted the Buddha into their hearts, and Buddhism was, in fact, the only important foreign influence in China until the nineteenth century. Buddhist stories have fascinated the Chinese public since Tang days. Buddhist words have crept into the Chinese popular vocabulary. The Empress Dowager was respectfully called the " Old Buddha " and a lovely chubby baby is called a " little Bodhisattva " (*pusa*). Indian monks came to China from at least the fourth century; they are called *shiseng*, or " western priests," and the Buddhist paradise is called the *Shitien*, or " Western Heaven." Already in the time of Jenghiz Khan himself, Peihai was associated with the great Taoist monk, Chiu Chuchi, alias Changchun, who was then living in the Kunlun mountains. When Jenghiz Khan heard of his reputation, he sent for him. Chiu went to Karakorum to see him, but finding that the Khan had left, he went on and the two finally met on the borders of India, after Chiu had met with the strangest adventures during the long journey. He advised the great Khan above all not to kill. Later he returned to China and was given a place in the Peihai area to live. The dagoba, however, was built by the first Manchu emperor, Shunchy, in 1652, in honour of the Dalai Lama's visit to Peking—probably as much a political as a religious gesture. Up above, close to the base of the dagoba is a shrine containing an idol with seven heads, thirty-four hands, sixteen feet and a necklace of human skulls which clearly indicates lama influence.

Standing on top of this Emerald Island one obtains a vision of beauty such as is seldom vouchsafed to the eyes of man, with extensive views of the distant countryside and in the foreground visions of imperial splendour. There is a twelfth-century description of this island, by Chou Hui, and another in *Chuo-kenglu*, in the account of the ancient glory of the Mongol period. Below lie the lakes scintillating in golden ripples, and in the distance, the Western Hills recede in diminishing tones of grey toward the horizon. On sunny days those same hills reflect the morning sun, which turns their red earth into a soft purple, changing into mauve and blue in the higher peaks beyond. In front and below, fantastic shapes of roof corners appear among the green foliage, and vermilion pillars covered with gilt tracings contrast pleasantly with the knotty trunks of

53. *Kuan* vase of Bronze *Hu* form, with a poem by the Emperor Chienlung incised inside the mouth. Height 9.8″.

54. Gourd vase of *kuan* ware, southern Sung Dynasty.

55. Portrait of Kublai Khan.

56. Detail from ' The Eight Officials': attributed to Chen Hung, active 730, but of the Five Dynasties or Northern Sung periods. Colour on silk, 9⁷/₈″×32³/₈″.

57. ' The Emperor Ming-huang's Journey to Shu ': detail from hanging scroll by an anonymous painter, ink and colours on silk; probably an eleventh-century copy of an eighth-century composition.

53
54

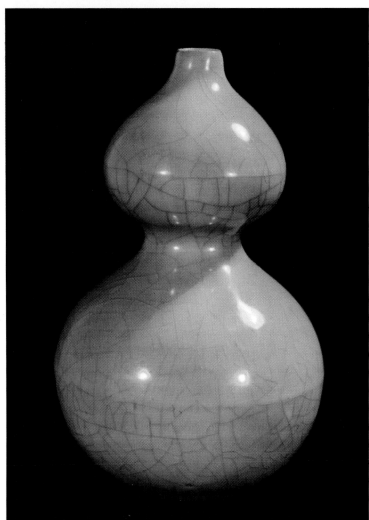

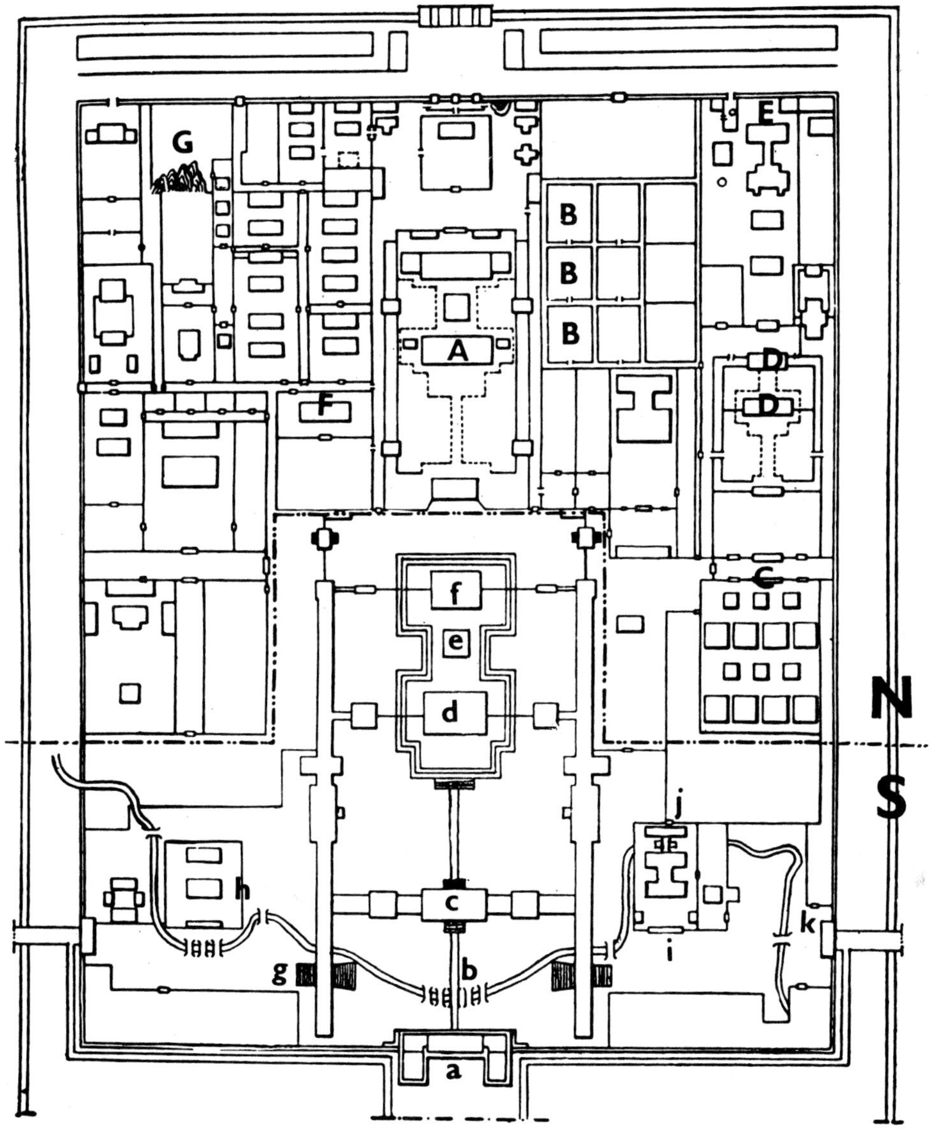

THE FORBIDDEN CITY

(THE NORTHERN PART OR WINTER PALACE)

A Chienchingkung
BBB Princes' Residences
C Nine Dragon Screen
DD Residence of Chienlung after retire-
ment and of the Dowager Empress
E Pearl Consort's Well
F Yangshintien
G Garden

(THE SOUTHERN PART)

a Wumen
b Gold Water Stream
c Taihomen
d Taihotien
e Chunghotien
f Paohotien
g Shihuamen
h Wuyingtien
i Wenhuatien
j Wenyuanko (Imperial Library)
k Tunghuamen

58. *Tzu-chou* type black jar
with relief in white
(Ming Dynasty).
Height 6³/₄".

the sophora and white pine. Here and there on the banks, *pailous*—archways with tiled, coloured roofs—stand at corners on the shores, and the marble bridges span the blue waters of the lakes. In high summer, the lakes are likely to be covered with miles of lotus blossoms, their subtle perfume missed by those who hurry past, but wafted to those who idle in the boats, or on the banks. To the east, in the immediate foreground are visible the roofs of the Inner Palace, as well as those of the three great ceremonial halls.

At different levels, especially on the north side, the hill is provided with pavilions, halls, archways, caves and tunnels, and the stone paths lead one to various unexpected vantage points. Down on the water level, the north end is bordered with a verandah, now not too well kept. I remember eating on this verandah a kind of Chinese corn muffin as it was made in the imperial kitchen (the Peihai was thrown open to the public in 1925). This *wowotou* is made of Chinese maize, or *yumi*. It is considered poor man's food, eaten by farmers who cannot afford rice. In the hands of imperial cooks it became a delicacy to be enjoyed for its very grittiness.

On the north side of the lake, opposite the dagoba, are two structures, one of which is of real beauty. This is the Chiulungpei, or Screen of Nine Dragons, which, as I remember, is perhaps thirty to forty feet long. It is all set with dragons and clouds in relief made of tiles of striking colours. Such a nine-dragon screen exists also in the Inner Court, on its east side, but that was rarely seen by the public. There are two temples of very unusual construction, the Little Western Paradise and the Big Western Paradise, all at the extreme northwest corner of the lake. The Big Western Paradise consists of a small hill of plaster, perhaps forty feet high, and on this plaster hill are hundreds of engraved figures of Buddhist saints. It is a sight to overwhelm the faithful rather than to inspire admiration. I felt a slight sense of horror such as one feels when looking at a collection of figures at Angkor-Vat or at Hindu Jain temples; every corner of the structure is filled with human figures. Sometimes I see tendencies of what I may call Chinese rococo, a tendency toward over-ornamentation. This is the case where in a Chinese garden there are too many windows and doors of various shapes, and ordinary walls have wavy lines on top. The classic beauty of simple lines is then forgotten. Likewise, ornamentation in polychrome porcelain can be and sometimes has been carried too far; nothing yet has surpassed the simple beauty of the white monochrome porcelain vases of the Sung period.

In Chinese gardens, the pavilion always plays an important role. A pavilion is a small, simple structure whose contour can be taken in at a glance. It must stand by itself as a thing of beauty, like a vase. Much ingenuity has gone into the modification of pavilions by changing their shapes and proportions and colouring their upturned roofs. Ideally, the colours and the general contour, whether square and solid and well-proportioned, or slim and elegant, must be chosen for a specific purpose. The matching of colours and shapes where several stand together is important. We see two examples of this in this area.

First, there is a Five-Pavilion Bridge, also situated at the northwest corner. The bridge, in the shape of an undulating dragon, is built into the water, and the five pavilions are placed almost in a semi-circle, connected as usual by corridors. It forms a charming little group by itself to break the monotony of the shoreline.

A better group of pavilions is seen on the ridge of Coal Hill, a short distance from the northern entrance of the Peihai. Coal Hill, mentioned in Chapter 3, towers perhaps three hundred feet high directly in the centre behind the Inner Court but separated from it. Thus it lies in a straight line with the many central city gates, beginning from the south gate of the Outer City. As there is no centre gate on the north, Coal Hill stands as the terminal of the line. Doubtless it served

59. Celadon dish: Yuan Dynasty.
Diameter 13¹/₄".

108

59

60

as a point from which to watch the bonfires from the signal towers. These signal towers, which were a regular system of warnings in times of war, formed a chain across the whole country from the region of the Great Wall on the north. The five pavilions on the ridge, arranged symmetrically as they descend to the lower level, have always elicited the greatest admiration for their shapes and colour. According to Juliet Bredon, [19] the fame of these pavilions reached the ears of Catherine the Second of Russia through the descriptions of her ambassadors, so that she ordered one of them to be copied for her palace at Tsarskoe Selo.

Down below, a tree with an iron chain marks the spot where the last emperor of the Mings hanged himself when the rebel troops of Li Tsecheng entered Peking. " At early dawn the emperor changed his apparel and removed his long imperial robe. The bell rang in the palace for the morning audience but none attended. The emperor then donned a short, dragon-embroidered tunic and a robe of purple and yellow, and his left foot was bare. Accompanied by one faithful eunuch, Wang Chen-en, he left the palace by the gate of Divine Military Prowess and entered the Coal Hill enclosure. Gazing sorrowfully upon the city he wrote on the cuff of his sleeve a valedictory decree: ' I, feeble and of small virtue, have offended against Heaven: the rebels have seized my capital because my ministers deceived me. Ashamed to face my ancestors, I die. Removing my imperial cap and with my hair dishevelled about my face I leave to the rebels the disarmament of my body. Let them not harm my people.' Then he strangled himself in the pavilion known as the Imperial Hat and Girdle Department and the faithful eunuch did likewise. [20]

The Summer Palace has the same basic landscape setting as the Sea Palaces, among hills and water, well furnished with towers and temples and winding corridors, but on a much larger and more expensive scale. It is a fact of history that this was the " $ 50,000,000 whim of an old woman ", that the Empress Dowager appropriated the 24,000,000 taels from the Budget earmarked for building a modern Chinese Navy and directed it to be used for the building of this huge pleasure ground for her enjoyment.

It is sometimes stated that China paid dearly for this in the naval defeat suffered at the hands of Japan in 1894, which entailed the cession of Formosa to Japan. I doubt it. Even if China had built a baby navy, it would not have lasted half an hour when the war broke out at sea. The suggestion that the navy funds should be diverted was approved by the Empress's chief adviser, the famous Li Hungchang. Given the state of affairs in the government of those times, it was impossible to have a decent navy. Li Hungchang's hand was in everything from coal and iron mines to steam navigation. He and Sheng Shüanhuai were among the richest men of that generation. The corruption of their China Steam Navigation Company was notorious. It was partly on account of the public outburst against the notorious Sheng that the Chinese Revolution of 1911 broke out. If those men could not run a commercial navigation company successfully for profit, how could they run a navy? At Tientsin, the Allied troops were to find about one million pounds of ammunition and a miscellaneous collection of rifles and shells brought for the profit of the compradores from Russian, German, French, English and Czech firms, with no reference to the actual weapons to be used. One Chinese gunboat was caught in battle with only two shells. How could China have won the naval war against Japan even if the money had not so been diverted by the selfish old woman? In 1900 the Allied soldiers tried partially to destroy the Summer Palace but at least they could not sink it. After a few years it was restored to its old glory.

There exists a scroll celebrating the 60th birthday of Emperor Kangshi, which gives a good panoramic view of the capital during the heyday of its glory. It

60. 'The Birds and the Flowers cut silk; Sung Dynasty.

III

leads the spectator from a view from the Inner Palace, through scenes on the northwestern part of the city, and passing the Shichymen Gate, through the northwestern suburb to end in the gates outside the Old Summer Palace. The scene showed the celebrations on that great day. There was scene after scene of troop formations, of cavalry, of the imperial carriage and escort itself, of the Manchu bannermen gathered at different points, of acrobats and musicians, and finally of the stations of welcome occupied by different provincial guilds along the way in the western suburb. The inscriptions record that this theatre was provided by a certain guild or ministry, and that by another.

The Yihoyuan is the new Summer Palace. Its site abuts on the ruins of the old Summer Palace (Yuanmingyuan). The sack of this happened during the reign of Shienfeng, when the well-known Empress Dowager was still a young woman. She shared with her royal husband the ignominious flight to Jehol. The memory must have festered in her mind like a sore wound. She had seen the Old Summer Palace in all its glory, now lying completely in ruins seemingly beyond repair. The vandalism had been thorough. So in her old age she thought she would build a new one for her pleasure, and this became the present Summer Palace. She was so delighted with it that after it was completed she spent most of her days in this new pleasure area.

The Summer Palace, from an architectural point of view, does represent the Chinese dream of an earthly paradise. It is sometimes called Wanshoushan, from the hill which dominates the whole place. It is situated at the foot of the Western Hills, near the Jade Fountain Hill. The buildings, hall after hall at successive levels, cluster around the eastern entrance leading toward the north bank where the great Foshiangko, or Buddha Fragrance Tower, rises high and handsome against the sky on the top of the hill. This represents best the Chinese idea of " ko," a tower built on a height for gaining distant view. Among innumerable structures, it has a three-storied theatre, a court and pavilion with an iron Tibetan prayer wheel, a wonderful living quarter for the Empress, fronted by a beautiful stone yard, decorated with a pair of bronze cranes and other creations. Great ingenuity was exercised in capturing views from a certain angle and level. Like the idea of modern landscape windows, towers and terraces were selected where the views of foreground and distant background merged into a harmonious whole. At different points, the white marble pagoda of the Jade Fountain Hill comes into view, so that one can see the whole scene with the white marble *pailou* in the distance as if in a dream.

At a lower level, a beautiful archway stands on the bank, flanked by two famous and very ancient bronze lions, and the whole shoreline is fringed by a long series of marble balustrades and a long, winding, painted gallery, famous for its beauty. Standing at the archway one sees across the lake the Lungwang-tao, Island of the Dragon King, connected with the mainland by the Seventeen-Arch Bridge, and farther out, at an angle, lies the famous and extremely graceful bridge, variously called the Camel Back Bridge or the Hunchback Bridge·

The big stone boat, *shihfang*, two stories high and some eighty feet long, is not movable and is set in water, as it were, for novelty. At one time the Empress Dowager introduced a toy steamboat to ply the lake, whose circumference is four miles. However she gave it up—probably she could not obtain the spare parts!

61. ' Pipa (fruit) and Monkey ':
    Sung Dynasty painter.

地行不
識名和
姓大江
高陽一
酒徒應
曳瑤臺
仙宴罷
淋漓襟
袖尚模
糊關

STUDIES IN FORM:
TEMPLES, PAGODAS
AND THE PLASTIC ARTS

COLOUR, form, line and atmosphere are the basic materials of all art, and the business of art is to create beauty. All art appeals directly to the senses, but atrophy of sensuous emotion often leads art astray to intellectual or geometrical analysis as a substitute and a gesture of despair. Any theoretical justification of such art is pure gibberish.

The exquisite colouring of the palaces and Imperial pleasure grounds has already been mentioned, but in all Chinese buildings, whether palace or pagoda, form is equally important. In all Chinese temple complexes the pagoda is a most important element—in the oldest temples it is indeed often the only part which has survived. It reminds one of a vase, standing in isolation and relying on line and proportions for its basic beauty. Just as in western cities church spires provide landmarks, so in the Chinese landscape pagodas serve the same function.

Peking is a city of temples, Confucian, Taoist, Buddhist and Lama Buddhist. On account of its perfection of form the Temple of Heaven stands out as the finest of them all. It has led writers to claim that it is " the noblest example of religious architecture in the whole of China," " a triple-roofed, azure-tiled, gold-capped shrine," and " a masterpiece of human inspiration." It deserves its reputation as probably the most beautiful single piece of creation in all China, greater even than her pictorial art. Its total emotional impact on the spectator comes from its majesty, its perfect proportions and colour and its harmony with the azure sky above, coupled with the religious awareness of monotheistic worship which it inspires. Juliet Bredon has recorded her feeling on seeing the Temple of Heaven in the following passage of great poetic sensibility:—

" In this quiet corner where the casual tourist so seldom penetrates we can gaze with no fear of interruption over the acres of waving grass and stately trees intersected by marble avenues, absorbing the restful stillness of all this plenitude of space and light and air. Let us return, if time be given us, in the early morning when the light is pale and the roofs hang like a faint, faint vision in milky atmosphere soft as memory, and again at high noon when the full splendour of heaven kindles and sparkles, and yet again when the sun is sinking like a fiery ball behind the Western Hills, touching the marble till it blushes. Let us stand once more on the altar in the magic moonlight, or when the powdery flakes of snow descend with fairy, transforming touch. When we have seen the Temple of Heaven in many moods, then and only then will we appreciate the full harmony of proportions in the blending of human architecture with the

62. ' Ink-Splash Recluse ':
Liang Kai;
Sung Dynasty.

115

beauty of trees and the spaciousness of the sky, and how truly it reflects life and life everlasting. Then we will feel that the sacred groves and buildings stand for wisdom, love and reverence and an all-pervasive peace that tempers the divine radiance to man's benighted understanding." [21]

The Temple of Heaven is at its most impressive by moonlight, for then the sky seems close and the majestic dome merges with the elements of nature which surround it. The gilt ball at the top glitters softly against the clouds, or against the stars in the blue sky; the triple roofs seem even more serene at night, benign but awesome. The white circles of marble balustrades support and elevate the whole structure—an offering of the human spirit to heaven. This is perhaps the world's finest architectural tribute to the spirit of nature worship, and, unlike the brooding palaces or graceful pavilions, the Temple of Heaven truly inspires as Gothic cathedrals inspire.

There is no more august ceremony of worship than the worship of Heaven. This privilege was reserved for the emperor alone. In it he acted as High Priest and Intercessor for his people. The sentiment is among the most ancient of all Chinese ways of thought; it is neither Confucian, nor Taoist, nor Buddhist, but antedates all of them. The worship of a monotheistic god, *Shangti* (the Chinese word for God) [22] goes back to the early beginnings of Chinese history. Confucianism was a system of ethical teachings, embodying certain social institutions based on history, and Confucius himself was essentially a historical scholar. One of the particular objects of his research was to study the ancient forms of the worship of Heaven in the millennia before him. Twice it was recorded in the *Analects* that he regretted that " there is not enough historical evidence," and " I do not know its details, because the historical evidences are not adequate; if they were, I would be able to establish them." Again he said that he did not know the sacrifices at the worship of Heaven; but if one knew, " it would be as easy to govern the world as to turn the palm of one's hand."

Nevertheless, the ceremonies of the worship of Heaven were not interrupted for four thousand years. The august feeling that it inspires is due to the fact that Heaven is the only God before whom the emperor bends his knee (outside his ancestors) and that this is the only time when he faces north to worship instead of facing south to receive worship. There is also the very old doctrine that an emperor rules by a " mandate from Heaven," that he rules only so long as God permits him, and that when a dynasty falls it is because God has passed the " mandate " to another. When a man succeeded in unifying the empire after chaos, it was taken as a sign that God had passed His mandate to him. For this reason, the term for " revolution " in Chinese is *kehming* or " change of mandate." It is the same as the European idea that a king rules " by the grace of God."

Other beliefs followed on this. A famine or drought was regarded as a sign from Heaven that God was displeased. Consequent on this idea, it was felt that if there were upsets in the elements, such as an eclipse or a drought, or chaos in the country, the ruler was to blame. According to Chinese mythology, as early as the eighteenth century B. C. Emperor Tang offered a prayer for the forgiveness of his people's sins and took upon himself all the blame: " If somebody should be punished, let it be me."

This basic way of thought became involved with the old Chinese philosophy of *yin* and *yang* and the " Five Elements." According to this theory, peace in the world depended upon the harmony of *yang* and *yin*, the positive and the negative polarities of the universe. If there was bloodshed and slaughter and cruelty in human affairs, then the balance of *yin* and *yang* was held to be upset. The elements were affected and the result was drought, continuous torrential rains or the appearance of comets.

63. A Lohan from Chili Province;
Liao-Chin Dynasty,
in Tang style.
Three-colour glazed pottery;
height 40″, width 31″.

雷雨卷潭湫來如珠還浦奧

無礙天人爭挽留吾如龍出

鸛骨老凜然不知秋吾佳雨

日月轉雙轂古今同一丘惟此

　　　眉山蘇軾上

辯才韻賦詩一首

老謐次

亭嶺上名之曰過溪亦曰二

子成二老來往二風流因作

辯才笑曰杜子羡不云乎與

領左右驚曰遠以渡過虎

出入戟往見之常出至風篁

辯才老師退居龍井不復

There are two units in the Temple of Heaven: the Altar of Heaven, at which the worship was performed on the Winter Solstice, and the Temple of Prayer for a Good Year, commonly referred to as the Temple of Heaven. In this, the prayers for good crops were offered at the onset of Spring (*lichun*). The Temple for a Good Year, called *Chinientien*, visually dominates the Altar, but it was at the Altar that the " Grand Sacrifice " was made. The only official worship which compared with it in significance and splendour was that at the Sacred Mountain of Taishan, another prerogative reserved for the emperor. Not every ruler would undertake this ceremony at the Taishan if the country was not prosperous and at peace, and it was considered presumptuous for a mediocre emperor to do so. All the details of the ceremony were handed down through the ages and recorded in detail in the dynastic histories.

On the night before the Winter Solstice, the solemn procession began. This was one of the rare occasions when the Wumen, central outer gate of the Forbidden City, and the Chienmen of the Inner City were thrown open for the emperor's passage. His sedan chair, draped in cloths with designs of gold dragons, was carried by sixteen noblemen, preceded and followed by two thousand people, including the princes, ministers, selected officials, eunuchs, grooms and standard bearers in their colourful uniforms. The path through the Chienmen was sprinkled in advance with yellow sand. The procession moved silently in the twilight. Near the entrance to the temple grounds was the emperor's pavilion, where he was to fast and purify himself during the night. Tall lanterns, hung in a huge box on the southeast of the altar, shone through the night. The box was so big that it also contained an officer, whose duty it was to look after the lanterns. Soon after midnight, the emperor rose, made his ablutions and dressed himself correctly to await the hour of dawn. Finally all was ready. The ministers and princes had taken up their positions on the successive circles of marble-fenced terraces, the carefully selected bullcalf had been broiled over a grill in a green-faced furnace at the southeastern corner below the terraces, and the shrines containing the tablet of Heaven and of the imperial ancestors of the House had been placed in position. Then the emperor emerged and approached the Altar. First he prayed and rested at the small round tower north of the Altar, the House of the " Ruler of the Universe " (Huang Chiungyü). He then proceeded south and mounted the three terraces. He stood ready at the south on the middle terrace just below the altar on the top. Then began the ancient sacred music, performed on simple instruments, including clay pipes. On the same circle with him and at the same level on the east stood the shrines for the sun, the five planets and twenty-eight constellations, and on the west the shrines for the moon, the clouds, the wind and the rain. Close to him stood a prompter, a keeper of the prayer cushion, and a " censor " whose duty was to see that all was carried out according to traditional form. Behind and below him stood the princes, and on the sides at a distance round the circle, the representatives of the Board of Rites, and others. On the lowest terrace stood the dukes and the princes of lower rank and the singers, dancers and musicians.

When the proper time came, the emperor mounted and stood silent as a statue. He took up his position at prayer. In front of him, on the south side of the circle, was the tablet of Heaven. Below at a little distance to the right and left were arranged the tablets of the Five Emperors and next to them stood the officers in charge of the ceremony and the prayer. The Emperor intoned the written prayer quietly and solemnly and then returned to his place on the middle terrace. There were three services and after each service, music was played. When the bull had been offered, he descended and returned to his pavilion. Every element of ritual and form had been observed. Directions, numbers of

64. ' Playing Children and Pedlars ': Li Sung, Sung Dynasty.

65. An example of calligraphy by Su Tungpo, the Sung Dynasty poet, painter and famous calligrapher.

steps, numbers of balustrades, all were rigidly prescribed and all had symbolic meanings.

For this worship, the ordained colour was blue. The sky was blue, the colour of the enamel tiles was blue, the officers' uniforms and the emperor's robe were predominantly blue. The five colours, five elements, five directions (four plus the centre) all had specific meanings in the cosmogony of *yang* and *yin*.

Basically the Temple of Heaven is similar to the two lowest pavilions on the Coal Hill but its huge size increases its majesty. The line of its upturned roofs is subtly restrained, whence its classic beauty. In Siam and Burma, the idea of upturned roofs was taken over and over-accentuated. The roof corners turn up at a very sharp angle, together with other exaggerated aspects of ornamentation.

In Peking, there are some examples of Indo-Chinese architecture which came in with Buddhism and of these the White Dagoba at Peihai is an outstanding example. A dagoba is essentially a reliquary, perhaps the tomb of a priest, consisting of an enormous dome, capped by a small top of various shapes. A very large example is the Paitasy, or White Pagoda Temple, situated inside the West Gate (Pingtsemen). It forms a pair in size and height with the one at Peihai, but, due to its position on level ground instead of the top of a hill, is less noticed. It dates back to A. D. 1092 of the Liao period and was rebuilt by Kublai Khan in 1272. Like the dagoba at Peihai, it is shaped like a chianti bottle, with a firm base. Above it rises a structure of eleven stories, or at least with eleven lines of roofs. On top of this again is a metal saucer surmounted by a small pagoda which in ancient times was gilt. From the projecting roofs hung a number of bells. Kublai Khan was a devout Buddhist. It was said that he used more than five hundred pounds of gold and over two hundred pounds of silver to adorn the monument. Fearing that visitors might be hurt by things rolling down, he had a white balustrade of marble built around it, protected with a copper netting. The Emperors Kangshi and Chienlung kept it in good repair, but now the temple is very old and decayed, and its large court is used for one of the regular temple fairs at which old shoes, rusty scissors and even fruit and vegetables are sold.

Another form of Buddhist structure, namely the stupa, is represented by two outstanding examples: one at the Five-Pagoda Temple in the suburbs near the northwest corner, and the other at the Piyunsy near the Western Hills. The Five-Pagoda structure used to form part of a temple, but now stands completely isolated in the fields. It was the gift of a rich Hindu Buddhist who brought golden images of the Buddha and a golden "Diamond Throne" to a Ming emperor. The latter was so pleased that he allowed him to build a temple on this spot in the form of the diamond throne. The temple was completed in 1465. The base is a massive square foundation, fifty feet high, decorated with Buddhas in serrated lines and without any steps leading up to it. Above the flat top of this massive foundation rise five pagodas, four at the corners and one in the centre, each with eleven stories.

The stupa at Piyunsy was built by the Emperor Chienlung in 1748, and is considered modern, but it is perfect of its kind, and, with its row upon row of sculptures round the base, is in a much better condition. Chienlung built it because he loved this place and had his private palace here. The five pagodas set upon the solid base have thirteen instead of eleven stories. It is, however, possible to go up, and from its summit one can have a magnificent view of the surrounding countryside, with its white pines, and Peking city itself in the distance. One also sees in the neighbourhood another type of Hindu architecture called " dorchens," which are tombs of priests.

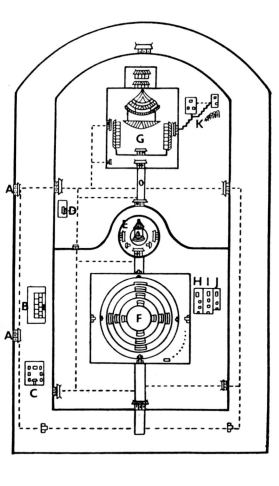

ALTAR OF HEAVEN

AA Entrances
B   Hall for musicians
C   Stables for sacrificial animals
D   Emperor's purification rooms
E   Temple to the Ruler of the Universe
F   Altar of Heaven
G   Temple of Heaven (or Temple of Good Year)
HI Deposits for utensils
J   Slaughter house
K   Covered passage

The pagoda is, of course, an intrinsic part of the Chinese scene. It is a kind of high tower (*ko*) narrowed down in width; but unlike the *ko*, it is not meant for residence. Its function is religio-Buddhist, sometimes modified by local Chinese beliefs. Though narrow, it is similar to a high tower in its number of stories, projecting eaves, windows and roofs. The windows have lost their function and are often blind, but their forms are still preserved. A *ko* may be one of several shapes—round, hexagonal, octagonal, and so on—and so may a pagoda. Sometimes bells are hung under the eaves, adding a decorative and rather feminine touch.

Very often pagodas are supposed to contain Buddhist relics (*shehli*) and Buddhist sutras were concealed in their foundations. According to Chinese native belief, they have the magic power of keeping spirits and demons under subjugation in their cellars. The Paosuta pagoda of Hangchow, dating back to the twelfth century, fell down in the first years of the Republic. It had been believed that the White Snake Spirit was permanently held subjugated under this pagoda, but when it fell, hundreds of small printed Buddhist sutras were found under it. As examples of twelfth-century printing, they fetched relatively high prices. As for the *shehli*, supposed to come out of the ashes when the Buddha's body was cremated, to the best of my knowledge, these were simply opals. The Indian priests knew this, but the Chinese did not. The iridescent colours of the stones certainly impressed the Chinese. I once had the special privilege, not accorded to most visitors, of being allowed to see one that was kept in a casket at a very old Zen temple at Kukong, north of Canton. The opal was offered with great solemnity for my inspection. The tooth of the Buddha is in Ceylon, but I have not heard claims that any of the Buddha's bones are kept in Chinese temples, only the *shhli*. The Chinese easily accepted this because it was natural for them to believe that Sakyamuni had for his bones jewels of such wondrous brilliance.

Of all the pagodas in Peking, the white marble pagoda of the Jade Fountain Hill is the most outstanding. Slimly elegant and resplendently white in the sunshine, it dominates the country from a great distance. Also at the Jade Fountain Hill is another fine example of a pagoda, this one being faced with green glazed tiles. These tiles can be very ornamental, like polychrome porcelain as compared with monochrome solid colours. Unlike other pagodas with regular intervals between the stories, this tiled pagoda has false stories of greater height, the lowest topped by double roofs beneath the balustrades of the second story. Of a slightly smaller width, the second story is again topped by double roofs, similarly capped by the rounded balustrade of the third story. This, in its turn, has triple roofs, is still smaller in width and is capped at the top by a large bell and an inverted saucer. The total effect is that of a crown jewel. There is a similar tiled pagoda, equally beautiful, at the Hunting Park not far away.

The pagoda at Tienningsy is one of the oldest structures in the whole city, dating back to the Liao period and thus antedating the Mongol dynasty. Some of the most ancient pagodas have disappeared, like that of the Minchungsy of the eighth century. In local songs it is renowned for " scraping the sky." The ancient pagoda of Tienningsy still stands almost immediately outside the West Gate of the Outer City. The Tienningsy is one of the focal points by which we are able to identify the ancient site of the Liao and Chin capital. However, its origins date back much earlier, to the North Wei Dynasty when in A. D. 472 a monastery stood here. Through the successive dynasties, it was built and rebuilt and its names constantly changed. It has stone carvings of the twelfth century and contains a huge Buddha. The temple was burned when the Mings captured the city, but it was rebuilt in the fifteenth century and enlarged. Chienlung rebuilt it at great cost in the eighteenth century. The pagoda used be hung with 3,400 little bells which tinkled in the wind, but most of these have disappeared. This and the Drum Tower built by Kublai Khan are among the oldest untouched monuments of Peking.

Peking has white, black and yellow pagodas. The Yellow Pagoda outside the north city wall is comparatively modern, built in the seventeenth century by the first Manchu Emperor to accommodate the Dalai Lama on his first visit. It has remained the seat of Lamas and Mongol followers of the Lama religion. Under Imperial patronage, it was several times enlarged. It acquired the adjective Yellow from the colour of the robes of the Lama priests, indicating that they were of the Yellow Sect. Again it has the Hindu-shaped top, and four columns surmounting it like the Taj Mahal, but of course on a much smaller scale. It is noted for its bas-relief, which is modern and therefore in good condition.

If one were to cut off one or more stories from the top of any pagoda, the resulting architectural form would be a " pavilion ", since pavilions can also have several series of decorative roofs. An extreme example is the broad, squat hexagonal pavilion in the Lama temple Yunghokung. (Yunghokung is called *kung*, rather than *sy*, because it was formerly a residence or palace of a Manchu prince.)

Another important feature of Chinese landscape, both in the cities and in the country, are the decorative archways, called *pailous*. The four great points of reference for the resident of Peking are the four *pailous*, the East-Single, the East-Four, the West-Single, and the West-Four. Their function is purely decorative. Two of the finest examples of *pailous* in Peking are the one facing the lake
at the foot of the palaces in the Summer Palace and the great massive stone *pailou* at the entrance to the Ming Tombs. The latter has been hailed as the

67

68

noblest *pailou* structure, partly because of its perfection of form, and partly because of its size. Size alone is, of course, no criterion, but the form and colours of this *pailou* are perfect. One of the beautiful sights of Peking is the marble gateway of the Jade Fountain Hill on a clear day. Though it is on a much smaller scale, the white stands out brilliantly against the surrounding green.

We have already mentioned the figures in bas-relief on the walls of the Five-Pagoda Temple, and those at Piyunsy and the Yellow Lama Temple which are in a better condition. The bas-relief of the Nine-Dragon Screen at Peihai, made of coloured glazed tiles, is admirable, though such work with the dragon motif is fairly common in China. The most notable example of engraved dragons is on the stone columns of the Temple to Confucius at his birthplace in Chüfu. These are also found in the "cloud pillars" (single stone columns—*huapiao* in Chinese) outside the Tienanmen, while those at the Ming Tombs are still finer. Next in popularity are the stone lions, which are very common at the entrances of temples and large official mansions. They have, however, by sheer repetition become conventional copy-work. For real original stone sculptures of animals, one has to go to Si-an to see the stone figures of horses at the tomb of the Han general Ho Chüping. This remarkable set of life-size figures is work of the second century B. C. One shows a horse astride a prostrated Hun, for these figures were intended to celebrate the famous general's conquests in Turkestan.

Bronze work in China dates back to the Shang Dynasty, some of it to about the fifteenth century B. C. Many bronze tripods from this period exist in collections, and of course the Palace Museum has some of the very best, authenticated by inscriptions cast in them. In Peking today may be seen the famous bronze horse at Tungyomiao (*see Chapter* 10) whose haunches have been worn shiny and smooth from the touch of pilgrims' hands over the centuries. (A touch on the horse was supposed to bring good luck.) There is the well-known copper bull on the shore of the lake, near the entrance to the Summer Palace. Here, too, may be seen two bronze lions of great age and value placed at the entrance to the Summer Palace, as well as lions at the great *pailou* on the lake shore on the Wanshoushan side. Both in the Empress Dowager's court at the Summer Palace and in the yard of the main palaces in the Forbidden City are bronze cranes and bronze lions.

The most outstanding piece of sculpture is the alabaster Buddha inside the Round City, at the foot of the White Dagoba Island in Peihai. Like other great works of art, it has captured a human expression in its eyes and smile and is known among westerners as the Jade Buddha "with the Mona Lisa smile."

Chinese images are generally made of wood or clay. It is an indication of the Chinese inability to take either religions or their gods seriously, that quite often one sees broken clay heads of giant Buddhas at the entrance to Buddhist temples. Such carelessness is consonant with Chinese commonsense about gods. The bigger and better endowed temples have a special hall of *Lohans* (Arahats, or Buddhist saints), sometimes as many as five hundred of them, always noted for their individual facial expressions. Because Lohans were unusual individuals, reputed to have supernatural powers, some assuming the guise of beggars, the greatest effort was always made to give them individual expressions. There are such halls of Lohans at Tungyomiao and at Piyunsy. The "Western Paradise" at the northwest corner of Peihai, mentioned in Chapter 6, is a mass of clay Buddhist figures but unfortunately it is without particular merit. A most highly valued image is the sandalwood Buddha, of great antiquity; this was formerly at the White Pagoda Temple and was moved by Emperor Kangshi to the Hungjensy at Peihai. It is made of such hard wood that it makes a metallic noise when struck.

67. A Buddha in meditation;
dry lacquer.
Yuan Dynasty.

68. A Kuan-yin, standing;
wood.
Yuan Dynasty.

The most notable series of stone sculptures of men and animals are those at the Ming Tombs, within a day's visit from Peking. These more than life-size stone figures of civilian officials and warriors in armour, stone elephants, stone camels, horses and others line the long approach to the tombs. As a broad generalisation the Chinese do not often bother with human figures and there are few such figures apart from Buddhas and saints which are of a religious character. For instance, there are no stone statues of any of the famous conquerors or generals, or of kings and emperors. It was just not the Chinese custom. The appreciation of the human body as such was never conveyed in Chinese painting or sculpture, and human figures in ancient Chinese paintings resemble potatoes. This, perhaps, makes them very " modernistic," for anybody can see the beauty of a beautiful pair of legs except the modern Western and the ancient Chinese artists.

The introduction of Buddhism into China gave a great impetus to sculptural art, and with it the sculpture of human figures: witness the great carvings in the cliffs of Tatung, about 150 miles from Peking, reached by going up to Kalgan in Chahar and them coming down to its southwest.

Already by the time of Confucius, in the sixth century B. C., Chinese civilization had developed arts and crafts using silks, jade, ivory, and lacquer. These are distinguished by one common characteristic, smoothness of touch. Today the best-loved Chinese gastronomical delicacies are those of a glutinous nature, which are soft and smooth to the throat. This, in another realm, may be due to the fact that the Chinese tactile sense was highly developed. Works in jade and ivory of the Chou Dynasty and Han Dynasty were of a splendid design and strikingly " modern " in their simple lines. Chou Dynasty ivories were never ornate or intricate, as modern ivories often are. The invention of enamel, with its simple beginnings in the Tang period and blossoming to full maturity in Sung, adds another category to those things that are smooth to the touch. It was principally because of Chinese silks and porcelain that the courts of Europe in the seventeenth and particularly in the eighteenth century so admired China. When Marco Polo returned with his uncle to Venice and showed his friends and neighbours fine Chinese brocades and velvets and said that silk was the daily wear of the Chinese, it had the effect of making China appear a land of fable. This greatly stimulated trade with the East and inspired Christopher Columbus's discovery of America.

The development of ceramics in China is worthy of a book in itself. Suffice it here to say that, to one of classic tastes, nothing can surpass the monochrome white vases and bowls of the Sung period (*Juyao*, *Kuanyao*, and especially *Ting-yao; yao* neans " kiln "). In this period the famous monochrome celadon, pale green in colour with faint markings, was also developed. Under the Mings, great progress was made under imperial patronage in developing pigments for the various enamel colours. The development of ceramics as well as bronze and copper castings under Shüanteh (A. D. 1426-1436), of *cloisonné* under Chingtai (A. D. 1450-1456)—*cloisonné* was known as " Chingtai Blue " in Chinese—and of ceramics under Chenghua (A. D. 1465-1478) was remarkable. When we come to the end of the sixteenth century, Chinese porcelain blazed out in many colours. The process of invention and perfection continued without interruption until Emperor Kangshi's time in the seventeenth century and that of Chienlung in the eighteenth, when imperial patronage gave artists a tremendous impetus to create works of great beauty and delicacy. The most famous of all is the " eggshell porcelain " and other Kuyuehshien wares of Emperor Chienlung.

69. ' Portrait of Ni Tsan ',
one of the great masters of
the Yuan Dynasty,
painted by a contemporary.

STUDIES IN LINE:
PAINTING AND CALLIGRAPHY

PAINTING is an effort to represent what is regarded as beautiful or of meaning in human life and the physical universe, in terms of line, colour, mood and composition. It portrays life both as it is and as it is not, for through selection and rejection the artist conveys the atmosphere, the meaning he wishes to express. He can transform something which is ugly or sombre in itself into an object worthy of aesthetic contemplation. In so far as the photographer also selects his objects and leaves some things out of focus in order to create emphasis, he too makes a selection, he too composes to create a mood and an atmosphere, so his art has the same goal as that of the painter. But photography should not be an excuse for the worker with brushes to avoid realistic portrayal of a landscape or a human figure, on the ground that the camera can do it better and the artist must avoid competition. This is a misrepresentation of the prime motive which should spur the artist to creation, which is that he should paint what he sees in his mind's eye and feels with his senses.

This problem of representational art is not new. The great Chinese poet and painter in the eleventh century, Su Tungpo, said that " Who discusses art from the point of view of mere verisimilitude talks like a child." The artist's vision of his subject, and his feeling for it, has always been the most important element, and his fear has been, not of getting too close to nature, but of being alien in spirit to it. As Su Tungpo said of his cousin, the great painter Wen Tung, when he painted bamboo he lived with the bamboo. He was in psychic communication with it. He swayed with it in the wind and rejoiced with it in the rain. Su said that bamboo shoots " sprout in my intestines ", and as he got a little drunk, out came the bamboos dripping from the point of his brush.

The basis of Chinese painting is, as all Chinese know, control of the brush-stroke, and this is developed through the artist's training in calligraphy. In China, great calligraphy is valued and esteemed as a work of art on a par with great painting. A few things must therefore be said about calligraphy itself, to show its relationship to Chinese painting.

The essence of the beauty of calligraphy is not static, but dynamic; it is the beauty of movement, not of proportion. The pleasure derived from looking at great calligraphy lies in the unconscious tracing of the artist's movements, although the final product must have composition, grace and strength. The best way to explain this is to say that calligraphy is dancing on paper, for in the movement of the stroke there are swift whirls, momentary pauses, lifting and sagging of

70. The Bodhisattva Kuan-yin, in polychrome wood; Chin (1115-1234) to Early Yuan (1260-1367). Height 7′ 11″.

shoulders, and long, masterly dashes in one direction. There must, too, be the speed and accuracy of the tennis stroke, for, just as the greatest tennis champion may, by the slightest falter of a hand, drive a ball out of court, so too the calligraphist may exceed the proper balance of composition by a millimetre, and even the average man—not just the connoisseur—can recognise it.

A most striking feature of Chinese calligraphy is its dislike of symmetry, because then the character becomes static and dead, deprived of the sense of movement. A film of a soccer player kicking off a ball will show that unless he continues to move forward he will topple over. So in calligraphy the curved, uneven lines convey the sense of movement. Thus the word for "not" (*fei*) originally meant "a pair of door panels", because the abstract idea "not" could not be conveyed pictographically, and the word for door panels was borrowed as a homonym. A pair of door panels are, of course, strictly symmetrical, but in any good calligraphy the balance is avoided by having one panel longer than the other, and often the two vertical lines turn away from each other at the top, to produce a lively effect. Thus one side becomes the elder sister and the other the younger one, and the picture becomes unified. ("Two sisters part in day-time and come together at night" is the riddle for a pair of door panels.)

Secondly, in a well-written character, the basis must be established. The basis must be solid and firm, sometimes in the form of a foundation or a frame, more frequently around a vertical axis. Lines, soft or strong, curved or straight, long or short, are then arranged round it. Space is thus properly arranged, overcrowding is avoided, and it does not matter at all if, in the piling up of strokes, space demands that the shape be oblong instead of square or that the central stroke comes down very long. In the calligraphic line, variation is sought in the distribution of large and small, heavy and thin strokes, so that the line as a whole and not only the individual characters should have dynamic unity.

Thirdly, and this brings us close to the technique of painting itself, the control of ink is of the greatest importance. Different schools are known by their varying uses of ink and stroke. Very often a comparatively dry brush is used (this is particularly true also of Japanese art), because the thin lines which it gives suggest clearly the direction and speed of the movement. Critics and connoisseurs of the work of famous calligraphers and painters, can recognise them by the way they lay their brush on the paper—whether it is *chung feng*, the brush coming down vertically, or *pienfeng*, the brush laid at a slant. Many gradations of style can be achieved with the various types of brush—either a stiff brush (made of wolf and chicken hair), or a soft one (made of wool), or any combination of these (for instance, a favourite combination is seventy per cent wolf and thirty per cent wool). Aesthetically, the effect sought is either that of rich, full beauty, "like that of a flower-garlanded young girl," or the dry, ancient look of a thin, rugged old recluse. These elements are known as the bones, sinews and flesh of a character. Heavily-inked strokes are full of flesh; in other types the bones and sinews are strong. These are the actual expressions and metaphors used in speaking of calligraphy. Later we shall see their applications when considering painting, especially in the portrayal of trees, rocks and hills.

Fourthly comes the fundamental law of Chinese art, sometimes translated as "rhythmic vitality", enunciated by Shieh Ho (A. D. 479-501) and never challenged. This rhythmic vitality, conveyed by lines that are *alive*, is of the very essence of calligraphy, as well as of painting. It is an axiom, attributed to the Prince of Calligraphy, Wang Shi-chy (A. D. 321-379), that every line must have three curves in it. And indeed that is no more than is found in nature. In children's drawings the legs and arms often appear "wooden" because they are too straight; children do not realise that all limbs have a built-in springing

71. Fourteenth century fresco of a magician laying his hands on the sun and the moon.

72

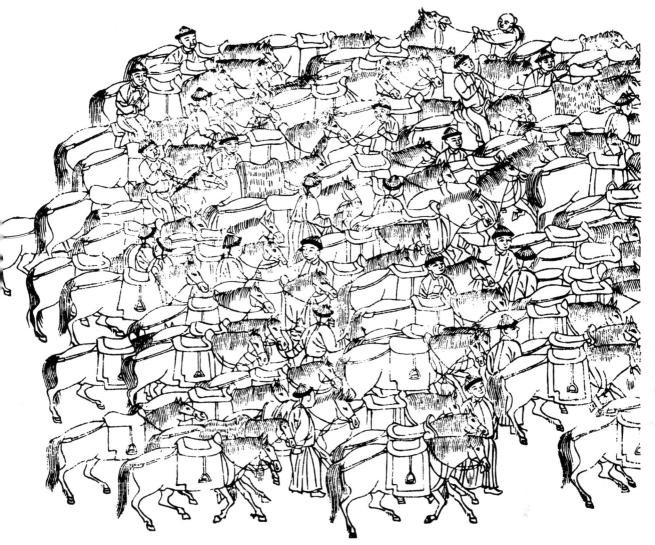

Horsemen, taken from a long series of woodcuts depicting in detail an imperial procession

movement, full of turns and curves. Wherever movement exists, in the sailing clouds or a running stream, an undulating line is always the natural result, and an artist should aspire no more than to imitate nature and be inspired by it. For this reason, Cubism with its straight lines is a horror to Chinese eyes.

Chinese painting has been broadly divided into two schools, Northern and Southern, the first consisting mainly of fine tracings, much like western mediaeval painting, and the second mainly of ink splashes. Very roughly, this also approximates to the division into " court painting " and " literary man's painting ". The latter is also known as " a play with the brush ", or " writing out a conception ", its essence being speed and spontaneity. It is this type of painting which is the most characteristically Chinese.

The subject matter very largely, although not necessarily, determines the style. Thus detailed paintings of interiors and of men and women in high society naturally call for painstaking tracing of outlines; it would not do, for instance, to have wobbly columns in houses. On the other hand, paintings of landscapes, of nature in all its aspects, need the vigorous rhythm of the calligraphic technique.

72. Picture in cut silk; Ming Dynasty.

133

Such is the Chinese artist's preoccupation with nature, in fact, that one finds an almost total absence of good portraits among their works. The so-called Chinese " ancestral portraits " are not known as that to the Chinese themselves; these were just pictures of men and women who could afford them, and were never meant to be works of art, as they were executed mainly by commercial artists.

Chinese paintings can be generally divided according to subject matter into the categories of *shanshui* (hills and water), *huahui* and *kuntsung* (flowers and insects), and *shynü* (men and women). Chiu Ying (A.D. 1510-1551) is the best representative of painters of men and ladies and the leisurely domestic life. Emperor Huitsung of the Sung Dynasty painted birds very well—perhaps because he ate so many of them. The eighth century painter Han Kan was famous for horses, but even he pales beside Castiglione's brilliance as an animal painter. The western artists' knowledge of anatomy and close study of animal forms, combined with a masterly brush technique, have contributed to the rise of the contemporary painter Ju Pé-on, who was educated in France. Another contemporary painter of animals was Chi Paishy (Chi " White Stone "), who often used shrimps, mice, chickens, grasshoppers and other creatures as his models.

Two early painters of the human figure were Ku Kaichy (fourth century) and Chou Fang (eighth century). Chou Fang's portrait of the poet Li Po is remarkable for its simplicity of line. The most famous Chinese painter of human figures was Wu Taotse, a Taoist of the Tang Dynasty. His work has survived in forms as varied as fresco painting in temples and in stone inscriptions. Principally he was noted for his swift, simple lines and the graceful folds of the gowns which his figures wear. In this he set a tradition. Where human figures appear in Chinese landscape paintings, they are invariably small and depicted with a mere indication of contours, produced by a few curving lines. The rules governing such forms were set out in Li Liweng's *Chiehtsyyuan Introduction to Painting*, which first appeared in 1679, and a most striking example of the technique is Shytao's painting which appears on the title page of James Cahill's *Chinese Painting*. It conveys perfectly the sense of " ancient and simple " (*kuchüeh*) which was the basis of the Pata Shanjen and Shytao schools, a style which has attained a degree of ultra-sophistication at which all sensuous beauty is rejected. Its development is like that of a man who has lived a fast life and known all the charms of women, but is now ready to enter a monastery and become a priest. He knows the world, but stands above it and detached from it.

In landscape painting, the variety of styles is infinite. As in calligraphy, when artists wished to vary their style or to create a style of their own, they did so by using a different brush technique, or by a different approach to portraying line and surface. In tracing chronological changes of style, there is always the danger of relying on artificial " periods ", of making a hard and fast distinction between " schools ". Really there is no hard and fast distinction between the so-called " Northern School " and the " Southern School ", or between the styles of, say, the eleventh and twelfth century. Students find such labels convenient, but artists themselves do not really know which " school " they belong to, or whose style they are following. Shü Wei, better known as Shü Wencheng (1521-1593), painted bamboos in the same style and with the same mastery of stroke as Su Tungpo, who lived five centuries before him. In Chinese art, affinity of spirit can count for more than coincidence of time.

With this qualification, it is possible to say that by the tenth and eleventh centuries, a perfect style with great delicacy and mastery of colours had already been achieved. Many creations had a rather conventional idea of surface, but showed great taste and dexterity in the use of colour—for example, the " Deer in an Autumn Forest " shown in *ill.* 39, or " Eight Riders in Spring ", attributed

73. ' Return from Stroll in Spring ':
Tai Chin.
An early Ming Dynasty
court painting.

74. Detail from
' Garden for Solitary Enjoyment ':
Chiu Ying;
handscroll in colour
and ink on silk
(Ming Dynasty).

75. Detail from
' Saying Farewell at Hsun-yang ':
Chiu Ying;
colour on paper.
Length 13' 1³/₄".

南羽寫此畫時在吾松為
顧光祿正心所作年三十餘故
極工妙自後不復能事多老
筆湯應如杜陵入蜀心後詩
吳君昌

to Chao Yen (tenth century). In "The Emperor Minghuang's Journey to Shu" (*ill.* 57), bold outlines combine with a strange, inspiring landscape to create a very striking effect. Painting in all styles, both in ink and in colour, flourished in the Northern Sung period, in the eleventh century. There was an extraordinary group of great masters, most of whom knew each other: Su Tungpo and Li Kunglin, the younger Mi Fei, and the Emperor Huitsung, of whom it may be said he created a fabulous garden and lost an empire. The genius of Su Tungpo gave great impetus to "literary man's painting", because through his calligraphy and his freedom of spirit, helped always by a little alcohol, he introduced the idea of the "play with the brush". Mi Fei too practically created a new style by using his soft ink washes to suggest landscapes submerged in mist and fog, with hill-tops barely visible in the distance and a few bare wintry trees, or perhaps a boat, in the foreground. He developed an approach in which he allowed himself to become intoxicated with nature. Once his love for strange rocks made him prostrate himself, dressed formally in his magistrate's gown, and bow to a certain piece of rock as his "father-in-law".

Immediately after Su Tungpo and Mi Fei (and his son Mi Yujen) came two great masters, Shia Kwei and Ma Yuan, who both lived at the beginning of the Southern Sung period, in the twelfth century. In these two contemporaries, a great style was born. Everything in the previous artistic development of the nation had contributed to it: the sheer, mystic joy in emptiness, the half-glimpses of distant views, the bold outlines of surfaces in hills and rocks. Above all, a new and rather more rigid kind of stroke was developed, so that lines tended to replace surfaces in importance. Strange to say, by emphasizing certain sharp, angular

Astronomica instrument

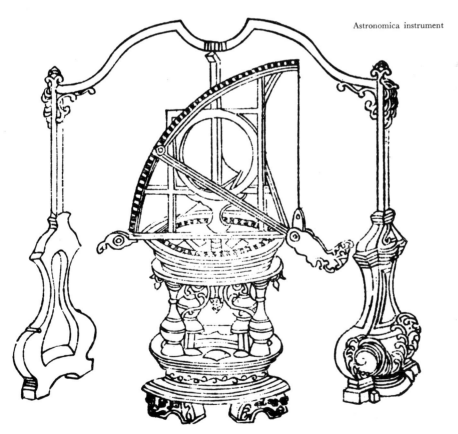

76, 77. Two details from a scroll showing various forms of the Goddess Kuan-yin.

天眼鏡

天體儀

Observatory

78. Detail from 'Spring Morning
in the Han Palace':
Chiu Ying;
ink and colours on silk.
Height 12″.

宣德二年
御筆戲寫一笑圖

79

lines and neglecting the actual surface, Shia Kwei produces a sense of looking further into the depths of things; even his waterfalls, dropping in conventionalized lines, give a strange effect of solidity. At the same time, his composition is perfect. His " Pure and Remote View of Rivers and Mountains " in the Palace Museum is one of the most admired of ancient paintings; in it one can see the birth of a visible technique. A similar style can be seen in Ma Yuan and his son Ma Lin.

In the sixteenth century, Chiu Ying and Tang Yin came very close to being " court painters "; they seemed to take great pleasure in depicting society and court life, homes, gardens, and in carefully arranging colours and details. While they show great skill, we miss somehow the spiritual excitement communicated by Ma Yuan and Shia Kwei. Shü Wei, on the other hand, clearly had a highly individualistic, spontaneous urge to create. His paintings and his poetry show that he painted and wrote because he could not help himself.

Then, early in the seventeenth century, a new, highly significant style was created by Pata Shanjen and Shytao. In Chinese estimation, these painters rank among the very greatest who have ever lived. Pata Shanjen was the poetic name of Chu Ta (1625-c. 1705), and Shytao was the poetic name of the monk Taochi (1641-1717). Both were scions of the Ming House, and both lived as recluses, perhaps in protest against the Manchu conquest. In these two masters, the brush stroke acquired a freedom and vitality of its own, and, in the case of Pata Shanjen, even a wantonness which suggests that the brush had taken over control and the strokes had drawn themselves, sometimes with a certain purposeful distortion, as in the outline of birds. Cahill aptly says of Pata Shanjen: " Whatever impression of laxity and clumsiness it may give must be understood as purposeful deception; no brush line in Chinese painting is further from true weakness. Where the stroke was made with a brush unevenly loaded with ink, marked variations in tone appear within it. Spots of ink are sometimes applied so wet that the edges blur as the ink suffuses outward. At other points the stroke is dry and scratchy. Through all this variety of brushwork runs a constant and very distinctive quality, which prevents Pata Shanjen's works from being confused with those of any other painter... They seem tightly disciplined, but by inherent and mysterious rules that have little to do with ordinary canons of painting." [23]

One feels that the contemporary master Chi Paishy has received the mantle of Pata Shanjen. Some of the strange drawings of birds by Pata Shanjen and Shytao appear to have given him direct inspiration. There are paintings of chickens, for instance, wich seem to be no more than haphazard blotches of ink, yet the chickens are extraordinarily alive, with a spirit of their own. In a way, it may be said that Chi and his predecessors developed an art-form which emancipated brush-work itself from the subject-matter of painting.

79. Dog in the Bamboo Grove ': Emperor Hsuan-teh (r. 1426-35).

143

LIFE OF THE PEOPLE

WE HAVE already briefly mentioned the hutungs, or alleyways of Peking. Hidden away from the broad avenues, but still within walking distance of the main streets, they provide much of Peking's charm. The broad open spaces of the city create the illusion of living in the country, especially where big trees cast their shadows on the yards and the twitterings of birds and the tap-tap of woodpeckers are heard in the morning. Unlike the main thoroughfares, the hutungs twist and turn upon each other, or lead unexpectedly to a square before some old temple. The rumble of traffic is far away; carriages seldom come through and only the occasional rickshaw penetrates them. Here and there a group of children play at marbles or a peddler beats a small gong to sell sweets made on the spot and blown and kneaded into shapes of chickens, lambs or other animals. All the houses are enclosed by high walls, doors are usually closed, or if they are open the inside yard is blocked from view from the outside by a green-painted screen.

The hutung names give the city its earthy flavour and its character. Their local names are always picturesque for they are given by the people who live in them. They are always in the local *patois*, with no effort at elegance — the "Lamb's Tail Hutung," using the *patois* Yang Yipa and not the more literary Yang Wei. Names like "Horse Tail Hutung," "Ox-horn Hutung," "Back of Bow" and "String of Bow," all describe the shape of the alleys. Others are equally simply known as "Sweet Well," "Wet Nurse," "Bamboo Pole," "Little Dumb Alley" and "Great Dumb Alley." Efforts have often been made to write them with more literary homonyms. Thus, "Great Dumb Alley" is written with the characters for "Great Elegant Precious Alley," which have more or less the same pronunciation. The "East River Rice Alley," which is the street of the Legations, becomes "East International Intercourse Alley." "Dried Fish Hutung" is written as "Sweet Rain Hutung," pronounced with the same sounds. Other names come from trade, or from shops well known for certain kinds of goods. Thus we have "Mr. Chao's Awl Alley," the "Lantern Market," and so on.

In Peking, it is difficult to tell the size of a house from the entrances for, as in many other Chinese cities, entrances are deliberately deceptive. Wealth is more often hidden than shown, a custom due to the old adage that ostentation invites theft. It is impossible to judge the size of a house except by the length of its walls, and sometimes by the tops of its curving roofs. Some have impres-

80. Turquoise blue jar with gold-bound rim, made for use in the Imperial Palace in the sixteenth century. Height 13".

81 82
83

sive red gates with gilt knobs and two stone lions crouching outside. But the majority of houses prefer smaller gates. Directly inside these is a screen, painted green, which shuts off the view of the interior from the outside. The fundamental idea behind Chinese residential architecture is privacy. A home is a place where one is with one's own family and close friends.

The plan of a Chinese house hardly ever varies. A courtyard, paved with stone or tiles, provides the desired cloistered effect of being in the open, yet complete privacy. Sufficient space is always available for a generous courtyard which according to the owner's circumstances is either decorated with rockery and elegant trees, or hung with clothes lines. But an earthen goldfish jar, about two feet high, seems almost to be inevitable. Simpler homes may boast just a date or pomegranate tree.

Each courtyard is a unit in itself, and a large mansion simply means a greater number of courtyards, connected with one another by roofed corridors, with a wall running along one side, and leading through a moon gate or a hexagonal doorway into another courtyard. A court is really equivalent to an "apartment," complete with sitting-room, bedrooms, study, and kitchen. Thus it is possible in China for families of in-laws to live together. They are all in the same household, share a common entrance, and although each unit is not entirely independent, at least the privacy of one sister-in-law is protected from other sisters-in-law.

In a Chinese garden, the aim is always to provide an element of surprise. It is never possible to survey an entire garden at a glance. The visitor may think he has come to the end of it when suddenly a door opens onto a winding passage through a rockery. Quite unexpectedly he reaches another small garden, with perhaps a cabbage patch, or an orchard with a small wooden bridge across a diminutive stream. Some wealthy residences are more elaborate, with stone pavilions and terraces. One has a pavilion extending on three sides over a lotus pond. This was formerly the stage of a theatre. The audience of family and friends could watch the show from a separate open hall directly opposite across the water. However, in the poorer quarters, several families must share the same courtyard. As the courtyard is always square or rectangular, the rooms are always identified as east, west, north and south rooms.

The people of Peking, some of them Manchurians six feet tall, have the strength, honesty and earthbound humour of the north. One sees in them a distinct difference from the soft, somewhat effeminate slick men and willowy-waisted women of Shanghai, and from the semi-brutalized rickshaw pullers of the same modern port. It is for this reason that many westerners have insisted that to know the true Chinese, one must visit Peking. There is no such thing as "true Chinese," or ethnologically "pure Chinese." All strains differ. As a native of Fukien on the southeast coast of China, I never regarded very highly the somewhat effeminate and indolent people of the Kiangnan region, in spite of their greater culture, but I have always intensely admired the sterling qualities of the northern Chinese. It may be that North China profited greatly from the admixture of northern blood, from the intermarriage of the Chinese with the Mongols and Tartars from across the Mongolian deserts. Otherwise, the race could not for so long have maintained its vitality. The northerner, in spite of all his culture, is still essentially a child of the land, robust, hearty and not a bit spoiled.

The tempo of life in Peking has always been slow and the essential needs of life simple. As everywhere else, there are slave-driving masters, nervous merchants, dirty politicians, but on the whole a down-to-earth view of life prevails. Its essence is reduced to a few simple factors, the bare, unambitious needs of a

81. A jade bowl with golden saucer and cover found in the tomb of the Ming Emperor Wan-li (r. 1573-1619).

82. The gold crown of Emperor Wan-li, which was buried with him. It is exquisitely wrought in fine filigree, forming a pattern of two dragons chasing a pearl.

83. The Ming Observatory.

A collection of musical instruments

happy human life—a good home, a simple way of making a living, family loyalty, a good bed and enough bowls of rice, some allowance for human foolishness. It is the old middle-class ideal of being neither too rich so that one becomes idle, nor too poor; a semi-humorous feeling prevails of being in the struggle for a living, and yet not engulfed by it in inordinate ambitions. This spirit, most difficult to put into words, is the spirit of old Peking. It created great art, and in a puzzling way it explains the gaiety of the Peking populace. In art, having come to grips with reality, the artist approaches it with a sense of detachment, of content, almost of resignation. Great artists have always insisted that the " ancient and simple " character is the basis of true art. The subject matter of art itself is revealing. In the previous chapter I said that Chi Paishy,

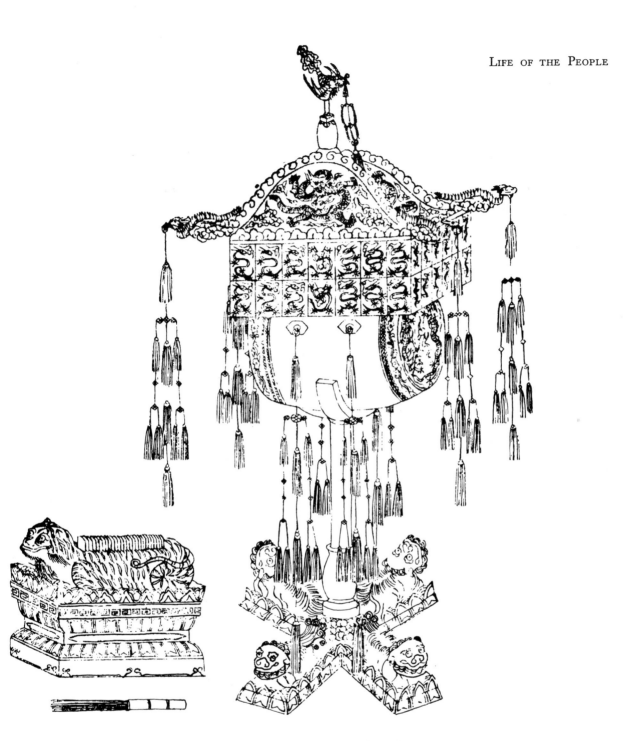

who died only a few years ago at the age of ninety-six, chose his subjects among the frogs, tadpoles, crickets, shrimps, grasshoppers, mice and carrots. This pre-occupation with the humble objects of life is most striking. The nervous struggles of a modern western artist to dissect and portray a fast-disintegrating universe are totally absent. That explains why, though the colture of Peking is so old, it has not lost the simplicity of thought and feeling which civilized man so often loses.

Marco Polo long ago observed certain innate qualities of the people, which have lived on through the centuries. " Their style of conversation is courteous; they salute each other politely and with cheerful countenance, have an air of good breeding, and eat their food with particular cleanliness." (I would qualify this statement if we think of cleanliness by modern and not the mediaeval standards of Marco Polo's days.) "To their parents they show the utmost reverence. Should it happen that a child acts disrespectfully or neglects to assist his parents when necessary, there is a public tribunal, whose especial duty is to punish with severity this crime of filial ingratitude." (This may not be strictly true today.)

Marco Polo also mentioned another habit of the Chinese people which is still widespread. "The present Great Khan has prohibited all species of gambling and other modes of cheating, to which the people of this country are addicted more than any other upon earth. As an argument for deterring them from this practice, he said: 'I subdued you by the power of my sword, and consequently whatever you possess belongs of right to me: if you gamble, therefore, you are sporting with my property'". This preposterous attitude ran directly counter to the genius of a nation which invented playing cards, chess, dominoes and mahjongg. The prejudice against gambling is based upon an entirely inadequate conception of the nature of life in general and of human life in particular. Kublai Khan could not possibly understand this philosophy of living. He failed to see that life itself holds many unexpected tricks, and believed that events would happen exactly according to the plans of man. Gambling is chance, but every player thinks he adds an element of skill. Human morale is bound to degenerate in a society where the state guarantees absolute security, where the element of individual enterprise, risk and chance has no outlet.

Like all other cities, Peking has developed the kind of entertainments which its people have demanded. The Northern Chinese have an innate sense of good cheer and fun, loving to laugh at themselves and at each other, and so the forms of amusement found in Peking are many and infinitely varied.

Simplest of all are the tea-shops and taverns, where a couple of pleasant hours need not cost more than a shilling or two. Song, music, women, boxing and acrobatics are provided in such areas as the Tienchiao outside Chienmen. Theatres are frequently in the open, or in yards where, as in the Elizabethan theatre, the stage projects into the stalls on three sides. The theatres are deplorable compared with modern establishments, but the singing is superb. Mei Lanfang and other great singers used to perform, not at a great opera house but in a small theatre inside the Tungan Bazaar, or at Kwangholou, where the benches were rickety, ventilation was nil and breathing almost impossible. But the surroundings did not seem to matter. There was noise and laughter in the audience; refreshments were served, and ushers, or more strictly waiters, sent wrung-out hot towels flying in the air across the heads of the audience.

The so-called *Chingshi* is specifically a Peking product. It is strictly-speaking opera, and not a play or drama. The difference between drama and opera is of course that one goes to enjoy the singing rather than watch the development of plot; one speaks of "hearing" *Chingshi* and not "seeing" a Peking opera. As in western operas, the plots are known beforehand and have been seen on the stage a hundred times. One looks forward to hearing a well-loved aria, sung as it should be sung. In the case of the Peking opera, the stylized movements made by the singers are just as well-known as the music. They comprise the measured steps (*taipu*), the particular gait, the whisking of sleeves, the rolling of eyes, the smoothing of beards, the different kinds of laughter, of cynical disappointment, or of an idiot, or of a wicked man seeing his victim fall into his trap, and so on. These are more or less mannered gestures and must be carefully studied, for the Peking audience is highly critical. Amateurs are booed, because the audience knows how an aria should be sung and how they expect a laugh to be made. The standards are very exacting. The Peking opera is not, as in

84. 'Goat and Sheep':
Chao Meng-fu;
Yuan Dynasty.

85. 'Ink Bamboo':
Li Kan;
Yuan Dynasty.

86. Detail from 'Scenes
in the Palace Garden':
Chiu Ying.

子昂常畫馬仲
信書米羊三百
羣滋寫一雙惟
具良通靈筆不
妙援華有誰方
豌乳富巾物伊
人寫玄長
甲辰新正月
渤毳 □□

87

much of the west, a form of amusement for the wealthy few, but, as in Italy, for the common people.

Thousands of opera lovers and amateurs exist who know the airs by heart. One form of maniac, not infrequently seen in the streets of Peking, is the " opera-maniac." He is mad indeed, but his lunacy takes the form of singing operatic airs in the streets. He expresses his sorrows, disappointments or grandiose sentiments by impersonating historic characters in public. He may believe himself to be a hero like Kwankung or a greatly wronged man, or even a deceived woman. Like all extreme forms of love, whether it be the opera, or cricket, or horse racing, it borders on lunacy. The opera addicts live by it. For their vocal training they go out to the city walls and do what is known as *tiao sangtse* (" lifting the throat "). This is always done early in the morning, particularly in summer.

It must not be supposed that the *chingshi* is the only form of opera enjoyed by the residents. On the contrary, if one went to the public amusement areas, one would find the *Tsinchiang*, or *Shensi pangtse*, just as popular. This music is characteristic of the northwest. Its themes are love and high tragedy, and the music is extremely high-pitched and sad. The Peking opera is itself the result of development and merging of two types of music, the *Shipi* of the province and the *Erh-huang* of Hupeh. The pronunciation of words is in an archaic accent, tinged with Hupeh dialect, and all singers have to learn to pronounce these words in their correct form. The opera incorporates themes from many of the most famous incidents of history, wars, separations and reunion, true friendship and marital fidelity. The theme of *Lady Precious Stream* for instance basically resembles that of Ulysses and Penelope: a great warrior returning after years of absence, tests the fidelity of his wife. It has also absorbed popular comedies from folklore.

There is also a closely related form of opera, the *kunchü*, or drama of Kunshan, near Shanghai. It is performed to flutes and a lower-pitched string instrument, the *erh-hu*. It is softer and, being from the south, always sentimental. As in the fifteenth and sixteenth centuries in the south the drama became a highly cultivated literary form, the *kunchü* is also generally more literary and requires a somewhat different standard of appreciation. Mei Lanfang is best known among the westerners as a representative of the Peking theatre, yet many of his sentimental plays, like " Heavenly Maiden Scattering Flowers " (*Tiennü Sanhua*) and " Yang Kwei-fei " (*Kweifei Tsuichiu*) are really in the music of *kunchü*.

As a metropolitan city, Peking is justly famous for its restaurants. There is no end to the books on Chinese cooking, but to my mind the Peking cuisine, as compared with the cuisines of other provinces, preserves the " orthodox " taste in cooking, namely purity of style and delicacy of taste. It keeps the original flavour of the meats, and does not indulge in fanciful gravies as Cantonese cooking does. As education should be the bringing out of what is best in a child, so orthodox cooking should aim at bringing out the best in every kind of meat or poultry.

The city has restaurants in the native Peking and allied Shantung styles, the best example of which is the Tungshinglou. Other schools of cooking are also well represented—the Szechuen cuisine, with its hot sauces and a very sophisticated, very cultivated style, or the simple earthy Mongolian style of *shüan yangjou*, large morsels of mutton plunged in boiling soup. Cantonese cooking never seems to thrive in Peking; the competition is too keen!

A few typical famous restaurants may be mentioned. First, naturally, comes the Tungshinglou, a Shantung restaurant of almost two centuries' standing. Situated outside Tunghuamen, it developed a cheerful " waitermanship " which

87. ' Chrysanthemums ':
Chen Hung-shou (1599-1652);
one leaf of
a twenty-leaf album,
colour and ink on silk.

A series of small gongs

is very important for a graceful and pleasant dinner. Here in earlier times the great officials had to pass when they went in the early morning for court audience, and here they stopped on their way out. The alert, courteous waiters had the gift of making the customer feel important, and the delicacy of the cooking appealed to jaded palates. When one ate *furung chipien* at Tungshinglou, one offered a prayer of thanks that the chicken had not died in vain.

Next in fame perhaps stands the Chengyanglou, famous for its mutton and its crabs. The crabs came from a special pond where they were fed with eggs. The mutton is a strictly northern dish; at the Chengyanglou it was barbecued in the open tiled court. The clients would stand around the grill, perhaps with one foot on the ledge, holding in a pair of chopsticks a very thin slice of mutton, which had been dipped in a specially prepared sauce, and eating it straight from the grill, with no loss of its full flavour.

Equally well known is the Peking duck of the Pienyifang, outside Shunchymen, which as a form of preparing duck has become almost world-famous. What goes with it is the not too humane force-feeding of the ducks. The birds are kept in the dark, and a kind of nourishing dough is forced into their throats at intervals, more than the animals really want. In this way, their weight grows faster and their meat is tender.

The Shawochü, near the West Gate, sold only pork and other parts of the pig and nothing else. Certain parts of the pig, like the snout, ears and tail, were of course limited, and after about ten a.m. the day's supply would be exhausted. Hence those who wanted such delicacies had to go there early in the morning Finally, there was the beef of the Mingyuehlou, on the Hupuchieh, served with a stock which has been in the house for a hundred years, continually replenished

The sporting pastimes of the Emperors throw a sidelight on the life of Imperia. Peking. All through the Sui and Tang and later dynasties, historical records mention a form of ball game which I take to be football. The famous Tang

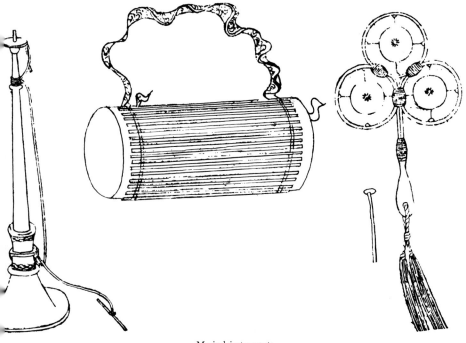

Musical instruments

Emperor Minghuang, husband of the beautiful and notorious Yang Kweifei, was himself a great shot with bow and arrow and also skilled at football. When he became emperor he promoted some of the young men whom he knew as riding and ball game friends when he was a prince. Tang earthen figures have been found [24] of a group of ladies playing polo on horseback. Ancient paintings show court ladies in the eighth century riding astride on horseback (see *ill.* 45).

Falconry was also popular, especially during the Mongol dynasty. Kublai Khan had his *Ing-fang*, Falcon House, in the western part of his palaces. The Mongol princes, too, all had their falcons, some big enough and trained to kill a young deer. Mao Tsetung, present Chairman of the Chinese Communist Party, mocked Jenghiz Khan in his famous and very revealing poem *Shinyuanchun* as one who " only knew how to pull a heavy bow and shoot big hawks." (He also states that the two greatest conquerors of Chinese history, Han Wuti and Tang Taitsung, who extended Chinese rule to the region of the Caspian Sea, were " lacking in romantic flavour "; " *If you want to see the great hero*," he says, " *look at this day!* ".) Falconry persisted into modern times. In the nineteen-twenties, when I was living in Peking, I saw Manchus, descendants of the early bannermen who came into China with the first Manchu emperor, who enjoyed this pastime and carried trained hawks perched on their arms.

Two other forms of popular sport are peculiar to Peking, the eurhythmic *taichichuan*, or *taichi* " boxing," and the shuttlecock. These are really forms of physical culture and there are shuttlecock clubs in Peking, like cricket clubs in England. One of the sights of Peking is to see a grand old man with a white beard playing shuttlecock.

Early in the morning both men and women can sometimes be seen having a short exercise in *taichi* boxing (Primeval Unity Boxing) under the old cypresses of the Central Park. The essence of this is slow, controlled and rhythmic movement, accompanied by regulated breathing. Instead of a quick thrust the

157

boxers give a slow, involuting rhythmic raising and stretching of an arm, and instead of a sharp kick, a slow, balanced, poised lifting of a leg. At the same time, the whole body, head, and shoulders move in harmonious response. It is, of course, more difficult to stretch an arm slowly than to do it quickly, as it requires more delicate control of the muscles. The regulation and control of breathing and expelling of breath are very important, and the exercise aims at toning up the whole system.

Other forms of popular amusement include the training of song birds and of talking myna birds. Homing pigeons are popular in the south, but not in Peking. In certain parts of the western city, it is not uncommon to see people gather around a temple square, each with a bird cage in hand. The birds are brought together so that the younger birds can learn singing from the others.

Cricket fights have always been extremely popular. During the Southern Sung Dynasty, about 1200, court ladies were so addicted to cricket fights that the sport became a national craze. The official history reads that when the Mongol captains reached the outskirts of the Southern Sung capital at Hangchow, the Prime Minister Chia Szetao was found playing with his crickets.

Singsong girls were always accepted as part of city life. In Peking, up to the time when the Communists turned them into good proletarian workers, a red-light district outside the Chienmen Gate was set aside as their residence. From Tang times onwards the court had always had its official musicians, as it had its painters, and the district of the musicians' court in the Tang capital is quite well known from Chinese literature. Many poets sang about them and many young scholars who came up to the capital for the triennial imperial examinations found themselves in love with one or other of these singsong girls. These fascinating entertainers sometimes changed their lives, influenced and even ruined them. However, strangely enough, sometimes the young scholars found among them true, devoted lovers who compelled them to work hard and sacrifice themselves in order that they might succeed in their careers.

The red-light district consists of eight alleys, known as the Eight Great Alleys, or Pata Hutung. For the convenience of the pleasure-seekers, the names of the girls in each house are displayed under a lamp at the gate on separate wooden signboards, painted in different colours. Thus there need be no mistake in finding " Golden Phoenix " or " Little Cassia."

These singsong artists form a distinct class and are not to be compared with common prostitutes. Their function and training are exactly similar to those of Japanese geishas. They are entertainers. Singing is their main accomplishment and some play musical instruments, but this is rare. In a society where wives did not appear with their husbands outside strictly family parties (birthday celebrations and so on) it was expected that men should seek the company of cultivated women and artists. These girls were sent for to grace a public dinner, like the Greek courtesans in Socrates' day. They stood or sat behind the guests at table, joined in the gay conversation, made a point of giggling or coyly covering their mouths with handkerchiefs, often helped in pouring wine, and were asked to sing snatches of opera named by the guests. Or men went to their houses, chatted for an hour or so, drank tea and cracked melon seeds and left. This was known as " going the tea round " (ta cha wei). Thus a man could visit quite a number of houses for the pleasure of being entertained by a number of different girls in one evening. The morality of these girls was about the same as that of modern night club entertainers. Fundamentally they " sell art," but " do not sell their bodies." They could and often did fall in love with their regular patrons and many married them. But a visitor had no right to demand closer sexual relationships unless the girl herself was willing. On a rainy, stormy

88. Detail from the Hall of Five Hundred Lohans in the Blue Cloud Temple at Piyunsy.

night, or when a guest drank too much he might be allowed to " borrow a dry bed " (*chieh kan pu*), that is, a place to sleep for the night.

When a closer relationship became established, more intimacy might be permitted, either because the girl loved the man, or because in the opinion of the madame he had spent sufficient money and given enough dinners for the house to merit the favour. On the other hand, a man who became an intimate of the house was supposed to the best of his ability to help pay, in a vague undefined way, the jewellery, dress-making and restaurant bills on the three big festivals of the year, on the fifth of the fifth month, Mid-Autumn and New Year's Eve. No fixed sum was laid down for this; a man had to gauge what was expected of him to repay his visits during the past season, and to ensure that his next visits would be welcome.

Ku Hungming, a great old scholar who was educated in Berlin and Edinburgh, once shocked his English readers by saying that if you want to see the true spirit of Chinese civilization you must visit the Pata Hutung and see the essential grace, courtesy and feminine dignity of these singsong girls, and in particular their ability to blush at obscenity.

The delicate matter of asking for payment is done in as inoffensive a way as possible. The madame would never think of naming a price for a night, and the girl would die of shame if it were mentioned. Instead, the madame comes to " borrow " money from her girl's friend on some well-known and well understood pretext, whose month and day can almost be told beforehand. This is typical of Peking.

Apart from the three great festivals, the madame, in consideration of your friendship for the family may wish to " borrow " money for putting up matsheds, *ta pengtse*, to keep the yard cool and shady before the onset of summer. When autumn comes, she may need to *tien lutse*, buy more stoves or repaper the windows. Whether in fact she actually buys more stoves is beside the point. Then there are always dress-making and jewellery bills, their size depending on the relationship and the resources of the patron. There are, of course, also " asses " from the country, who are personally boorish, and who, after spending a thousand dollars are still excluded from the girl's favours.

This may be an appropriate place at which to interject a note on women's costume. Western tourists tend to form their idea of ancient Chinese dress from the formal mandarin coat, usually of brocade in some shade of red and embroidered with golden threads. Any look at an ancient painting should dispel this idea. The formal dress put on when one was sitting for an ancestral portrait is one thing, the everyday dress is quite another. The ladies' dresses were not, on the whole, as stiff as the mandarin coat suggests. They were usually made of soft, clinging silk, with long sleeves and flowing lines. The collar, round or V-shaped, was extremely low. Beneath a loose gown, open at the front, was a garment corresponding more or less to the slip, or at least to a dressing-gown with an Empress Eugenie waistline. This is uniformly the case in all Tang, Sung and Ming paintings; Chiu Ying's paintings of court life and rich men's homes illustrate this particularly clearly. (See *ill.* 44 and 45.)

Ladies' hair was dressed in a high pompadour of infinitely varying shape, and studded with shining brooches of pearl, jade or gold, or inlaid kingfisher feathers. In the earlier Tang paintings, the ladies' facial contours (a full oval) and their hairdos recall the Japanese paintings of women. This is no doubt owing to the influence exercised by the Tang artists on the hundreds of Japanese students (mainly of Buddhism) who came to Changan in the eighth century.

89. 'Waiting for the Ferry in Spring': Chiu Ying.

BELIEFS AND FANCIES

ONE QUALITY of the Chinese people previously mentioned is their closeness to the earth. This is particularly true of the northerners. Their simplicity and spontaneity, gaiety and warmth are unspoiled by centuries of culture. Another aspect of this quality is a degree of primitiveness in their fancies and beliefs and a certain *naïveté* of thought. In their social dealings and the roundabout approach by which they try to avoid hurting the feelings of others, they may be far from simple-minded; a certain deviousness makes social intercourse and business dealings somewhat difficult. In this particular respect, the Chinese regards westerners' straightforwardness as "simpleminded." But in their folk religion, they do show a *naïveté* characteristic of man in the early stages of civilization.

This quality is revealed in the large realm of popular religion and the local pantheon and religious festivals. By popular religion, I mean religious beliefs which have sprung from the minds of the people themselves. These beliefs have nothing to do with the original teachings of the great religions. The richness of mythology in all ancient peoples and the death of mythology in modern man is an indication of the difference.

All peoples have, of course, created gods in their own image and according to their needs; in fact they want their gods to be the way they create them. An outstanding example is the popular Chinese Kwanyin, Our Lady of Mercy, Saviour of the Afflicted and Distressed, whom the Chinese created out of a Buddhist saint, originally a male divinity. The people needed a goddess. Early Buddhism omitted to provide one. Therefore the Chinese people created her. The popularity of Kwanyin shows how people needed to worship a gentle goddess, whose one aim was to succour the poor and the unhappy. And this goddess gradually acquired different functions according to the needs of her devotees. One particular Kwanyin had the special ability to give children to those who were barren; another specialized in curing eye trouble. When the people need such gods, nothing has ever stopped them from creating them.

Whatever Confucianism, Taoism and Buddhism, the three great religions of China, may have taught, the Chinese people are basically polytheistic, and to a very large extent animistic. It is easy for twentieth-century man to misunderstand popular religion, since he tends to apply standards of scientific truth to beliefs which spring from poetic fancy. Anything—a legend, a myth, a beautiful metaphor, even a pun—will serve to illustrate a truth. As with children, the imagination of early man was keener and more graphic. What to him was

90. Blue-and-white porcelain jar, fourteenth century. Height 14¹/₂".

91. Large blue-and-white porcelain jar, Hsuan-teh period.

162

90

91

true was often merely what pleased his fancy. This attitude is akin to the modern feeling towards certain superstitions, like Friday the thirteenth, or walking under a ladder. Few people would try to justify such superstitions, and most including those who believe in them, adopt a rather amused attitude of tolerant scepticism towards them. Nobody will swear that they are absolutely true. The attitude is rather that they may be true or that it does not matter whether they are so or not. The most that those who believe in them will say is " there may be some truth in avoiding Friday the thirteenth." Mythology was born when man's imagination was free, and his mind often poetic. What was felt as poetry was expressed in religious terms, until in later generations some scholastic minds made them into certainties, and found themselves in a great deal of trouble, as, for instance, in dealing with the problem of the origin of evil in the universe. And in a sense, it is a pity that this faculty of poetic fancy has died out in modern man, for as a result he demands that a thing be either true or untrue. There can appear to be no area in between. In a way, we regret with Wordsworth that we can no longer " have sight of Proteus rising from the sea."

This playfulness of belief is a particular quality of the Chinese mind. The Tibetans may take their gods seriously but the Chinese people never have. A few examples from local Peking beliefs are illuminating. There are nine gates in Peking; eight of them have gongs, but the gate near Hatamen has a bell. There is a well near the Hatamen Gate, and tradition had it that one day the dragon in the well would rise and cause a flood in the city. Consequently a stone turtle was placed over the well, the people promising the turtle that he need not worry, for when the gong was struck at night he would be relieved. By a ruse, however, the people substituted a bell for the gong, and the poor turtle has been sitting there for centuries still hoping that he would hear a gong struck and be relieved. How attractive is the fancy, but what has it got to do with scientific truth?

Another example is the stone tablet under the bridge at Chungkulou, near the Houmen Gate. It is associated with Liu Powen, adviser to the first Ming emperor and an astrologer, like Nostradamus, credited with supernatural powers of foretelling the future. He moved and lived in the world of necromancy and other superstitions. At Liu's suggestion, the tablet under the bridge was inscribed with the words " Peking City," as a method of outwitting the gods. If the gods should be angry and determine to drown the city, they would see, when the flood reached the level of the tablet under the bridge, that " Peking city " was already under water. They would then desist and be satisfied.

Another practice is that of gagging the kitchen god. Of all the gods, the kitchen god knows most about what happens inside a family, between husband and wife, parents and children, and so on. However, seven days before New Year, the kitchen god goes up to heaven for his New Year holidays. While in heaven he is believed to make a report to the Jade Emperor of Heaven about the secrets of the members of the family. This, of course, would be most embarrassing. Therefore, on the twenty-third day of the twelfth month, it is the custom to have a gluey paste made and smear it across the kitchen's god's mouth on the red paper image. Or else he is given sweetmeats, symbolically to suggest either that he will say " sweet words " or that he will be tongue-tied.

Two famous tales have been told involving local gods of Peking. One is the very beautiful story about Chung Niangniang, Our Lady of the Bell. Once Emperor Yunglo ordered an especially big bell to be cast. This may possibly be the one at the Big Bell Temple, north of the City, quite near Tsinghua University. According to Mrs. Archibald Little, it weighs over 87,000 pounds, and exceeds in weight the big bell of Erfurt and others.[25]

92. Red lacquer bottle
peony pattern:
late Ming.

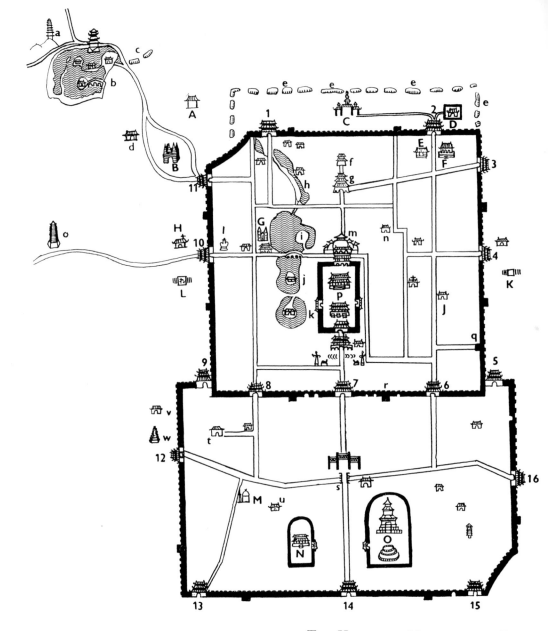

THE HISTORICAL MONUMENTS OF PEKING

A Great Bell
B Five Pagoda Temple
C Yellow Temple
D Temple of Earth
E Confucian Temple
F Yunghokung (Lama Temple)
G Peitang Mission (Catholic)
H Shala (Jesuit Tombs)
I White Pagoda Temple
J Dog Temple
K Sun Temple
L Moon Temple
M Mosque
N Temple of Agriculture
O Temple of Heaven
a Jade Fountain Hill
b Summer Palace
c Old Summer Palace

d Wanshousy
eee Ruins of Mongol Rampart
f Bell Tower
g Drum Tower
h Shyshahai
i Peihai
j Chunghai
k Nanhai
m Coal Hill
n Peking National University
o Palichuang Pagoda
p Forbidden City
q Observatory
r Legation Quarters
s Tienchiao
t Paokuosy
u Fayuansy
v Poyunkuan

w Tienningsy Pagoda
1 Tehshengmen
2 Antingmen
3 Tungchymen
4 Tungyomiao
5 Tungpienmen
6 Hatamen
7 Chienmen
8 Shunchymen
9 Shipienmen
10 Pingtsemen
11 Shichymen
12 Changyimen
13 Yu-anmen (Nanshimen)
14 Yungtingmen
15 Chiangtsemen
16 Shawomen.

The bell maker had never had the experience of casting such a huge bell, and each time it cracked when it cooled. He was in misery and feared the wrath of the emperor for his failure. He had, however, a sweet young daughter. On seeing her father's despair, she asked what it was that troubled him. That night she had a dream that if human flesh were thrown into the molten mixture it would prevent cracking and ensure the success of the casting. The following day, while the metal was boiling, her father left off for lunch. She seized her opportunity, leaped into the molten liquid and was consumed. The big bell was cast without a flaw. That is why today when the bell rings at night one is said to hear the sad wailing of Our Lady of the Bell.

Another myth is connected with the origin of the water supply for the city of Peking. As we know, the water of the Sea Palaces comes from the Jade Fountain some twelve miles away on its west. There is a bridge outside the northwest corner of the city, the Kaoliang Bridge, named after a eunuch who sacrificed his life that the city might have a plentiful water supply. Once there was a drought in Peking. The Ming emperor was worried over the shortage of water. He had a dream in which he met an old peasant pushing a wheelbarrow containing two hampers, and was told that they contained water for the city of Peking. The next morning he asked his astrologer the meaning of this dream, and the latter told him that the god had shown mercy and would send water to the city. The astrologer suggested that a man should be sent to the western suburb, armed with a sword, and that there he would meet a certain old peasant, carrying a certain pair of hampers towards the city. He further instructed that the man should stab the hampers with his sword and immediately turn round and run towards the city, never looking back. The man who offered to go was Kao Liang. He went and met an old peasant exactly as had happened in the emperor's dream. When he was told by the old man that the hampers carried "water for the city of Peking," he quickly ran the sword through the hampers and started to run back. Behind him he heard a tremendous rush and roar of water inundating the fields and coming rapidly towards the city. On seeing the gate tower of Shichymen Gate he thought he was safe and turned to look. Immediately he was engulfed by the onrushing waters. Hence the bridge is consecrated to his memory. It is clear that myths were still being created as late as the fifteenth century. Why is it that there is no myth about Big Ben or London Bridge? Is it because when we hear such myths we are inclined to feel terribly grown-up and sneer at such stories as "preposterous"? Suppose they are untrue. Who cares? Our life is the richer for them.

Thus we are not dealing here with the major religions of China, but with popular beliefs accepted by the common people. Of the major religions, Confucianism is rationalist and the least picturesque. The Confucian Temple in the North City is strictly something for the literati, and the tablet of Confucius behind the altar is no more than an oversized foot rule, inscribed with words making it a symbol of the spirit of the Master. Taoism has its deep philosophy embodied in the writings of Laotse, and Buddhism has its lofty metaphysics concerning the problems of knowledge and reality. However, the people are most interested in the gods of riches, of longevity, of matrimony, of luck. None of these gods inspire as deep a belief as the Goddess of Mercy, but the prayers offered to them are equally sincere.

The best example of the polytheistic beliefs in gods created by the people themselves irrespective of sect or religion, is the Temple to the Eastern Sacred Mountain, or Tungyomiao, outside Chihuamen, which dates back to the fourteenth century (A. D. 1317). The worship of Taishan or the Eastern Sacred Mountain is neither Taoist, nor Buddhist; it has to do with a basic cosmogony of

BELIEFS AND FANCIES the five elements (*wushing*), the five points, five colours, and five sacred mountains which was native to Chinese beliefs in the first centuries B. C. It is Taoist in the sense that popular Taoism has absorbed into itself all the native polytheism, animism, black magic and occultism. The gods of matrimony, of riches and of medicine are neither Taoist nor anything else. They simply fulfil a basic need. At this temple may be seen the god of matrimony, who is called the Old Man of the Moon. This comes from a tale of the ninth century about

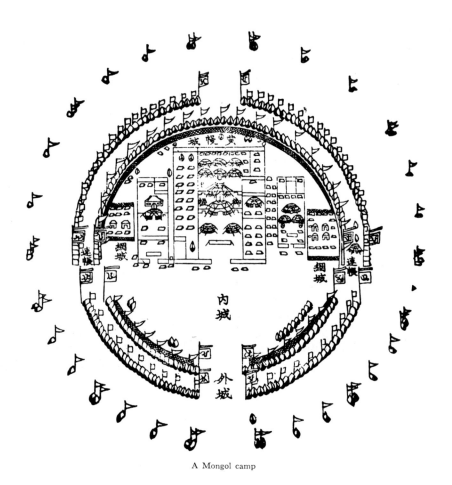

A Mongol camp

how all marriages are made in heaven, and how from the time a baby is born its feet are connected by a red thread with another baby of the opposite sex. No matter what obstacles and parental obstructions may be put in their way they are bound to end by marrying each other. At least one can go there, shake the divination sticks in a bamboo pot until one of them drops to the floor and from the oracular verse on it find out whether a romance with a certain young man or girl will succeed.

There is also a God of Literature, about whom the teachings of Confucius, Laotse, or Buddha say nothing. The God of Literature is a constellation of stars governing the luck of scholars at the imperial examinations. Then the gods' functions multiplied. There are gods of rheumatism, of fever and colic, of consumption and stubborn coughs, of toothache and cataracts and haemorrhage. It is interesting to note that the present Peking University occupies a site which is popularly known as the Mashenmiao, Temple of the God of Horses, or of the

93. Green celadon buffalo; sixteenth century. Length 12″.

168

Protector of Horses. This is on the East Side of Coal Hill, where in earlier periods the imperial stables stood. Another house, the Erhlangmiao, south of the Legation Quarters, opposite the Tengshykou or Lantern Market, is popularly called the "Dog Temple." This function of the god Erh-Lang (celebrated in the famous religious epic, *Shiyuchi*) was the product of an accident. A certain woman, while praying for the health of her son, went to the temple with a sick dog and on her return found that the dog was cured. Hence there are found at this "Dog Temple" *ex voto* offerings of small puppies placed at the Altar of Erh-lang, who was, like St. Michael, essentially a mighty military god.

Certain temples are particularly associated with specific religious festivals. The Tungyomiao, for example, on the fifteenth day of the seventh month, attracts a huge crowd of onlookers to watch the lantern boats. In spring, pilgrims come from as far as Changping and Chunyi to ascend the heights of Miaofengshan. They climb successive peaks, passing through Tachuehsy and the Black Dragon Pool, deep into the Western Hills. The temple has two attractions: the Kwanyin of Many Children (*Tsysun Niangniang*) and the Kwanyin of Good Eyesight. The temple is situated on one of the highest points in the Western Hills and commands a breathtaking view of the whole country around. But, if during the ascent one kneels down every three steps and prostrates oneself every nine steps, as do some of the pilgrims, the journey can take days, with overnight stops at one of the many temples on the hills. Such a journey is truly heroic, for the road is full of uncut rocks and the climb at places, especially toward the summit, is very steep. Many women are among the pilgrims, women who desire a son or have some other wish very close to their hearts. The idea behind the journey is not really to do penance. A prayer is but a fervent wish of the heart, and a fervent wish of the heart is a prayer. The hardship undertaken was a natural expression of the fervency of their wish.

A word may be said about Chinese adherents to other world religions. Mohammedans have always had a strong foothold among the Chinese population, and Mohammedan restaurants, known as *Ching Chen* shops ("Pure and True," the Chinese name for Islam), which sell mutton but no pork, are quite common in the streets of Peking. Chinese Mohammedans have an almost fanatic unity. Some forty years ago, a Peking publisher published something derogatory about the Mohammedan custom of not eating pork, and stirred up a nation-wide hornets' nest. It came as a great surprise to find that there were so many Mohammedans in China, not only in Peking but also in the far south and southwest. This religion came through Chinese Turkestan, brought by the Uigurs, Kirghiz and Cossacks. The local Turkestan population has always been largely Mohammedan, and bloody massacres of whole villages have often occurred between the Buddhists and the Mohammedans in this very large and little known region (Shinkiang province). As far back as the eighth century Uigur soldiers were conscripted and many settled in the northwest, in Shensi. Many of the Mohammedans in Peking without doubt are descendants of Turkic soldiers from that region who decided to settle in Peking.

Once there was a Huitseying (Mohammedan camp), now abolished, near the Shinhuamen Gate, just outside the Imperial City. It is connected with a pathetic story of a young and beautiful Mohammedan queen, who came from the neighbourhood of Kashgar. Her tribe was conquered by Chienlung's army, her husband, a Uigur chieftain, was killed in action and she was taken to Peking. There she was known as Fragrant Concubine, because, being of foreign origin, her body was said to have a special piquant odour, or, more courteously, as "Kofei," or the "Guest Concubine." The great Emperor Chienlung wanted to make her his imperial consort, tempting her with offerings of the greatest luxury. Fragrant

94. Buddhist figure; Kangshi period.

Concubine hated the man who had killed her husband and turned a cold shoulder toward him. Her body was captive, but her heart was unconquered. Chienlung was extremely patient. He built for her the *Wangchialou* (the tower where she could " look afar and think of home ") and facing it a whole village with Turkish tents and a Mohammedan mosque in order to alleviate her homesickness. But the young lady committed suicide rather than be unfaithful to the memory of her husband. The portrait of Fragrant Concubine by the Jesuit Priest Castiglione, now in the Palace Museum, usually attracts a great deal of interest as a result of this tragic story. He painted her wearing a helmet and Italian armour of grey metal.

Nestorian Christians came to China as early as the seventh century A. D. The Nestorians were a Christian sect which refused to accept the divinity of the Holy Virgin. Driven by persecution out of Asia Minor, they finally settled in Shensi province, as the Nestorian Tablet at Si-an, dated A. D. 635, testifies. Albert von Le Coq in his archaeological expedition sent out by Kaiser Wilhelm,[26] discovered also some Manichaean manuscripts in Chinese Turkestan in addition to sculpture which looked decidedly Greek. Marco Polo mentioned Christians living not only in North China, but also as far south as Yunnan. He mentioned also Kublai Khan's war against the Kingdom of " Prester John " (Priest John), ostensibly a Nestorian.[27]

Odoric, sent by a Roman Catholic Pope, also visited Peking shortly after the death of Kublai Khan. However, the Jesuit who made the greatest impact on the Chinese court of Emperor Wanli (A. D. 1573-1619) was Matteo Ricci. His great success was mainly due to the fact that he took the trouble to study the Chinese language and the Confucian classics, and was therefore accepted by Chinese scholars. He was a great favourite with the Chinese Emperor and converted an outstanding Chinese scholar, Shü Kwangchi. Shü's daughter also became Catholic and was known as Sister Teresa. When Ricci died, in A. D. 1610, he was buried with all honours by the order of the emperor. His tomb at Shala, about a mile from Pingtsemen, was desecrated during an anti-Christian riot of the Boxers in 1900, together with the tombs of two other outstanding early Jesuit fathers, Adam Schall and Verbiest. Father Schall served both the Ming and Manchu emperors, and Verbiest the astronomer converted not only many ladies of the court, but also almost succeeded with Emperor Kangshi himself. The Jesuits called Kangshi's empress " Anne ", and the Empress Dowager, " Helene ". Kangshi could not himself become converted because the Roman Catholics could not agree that ancestor worship, that is, grateful memory of one's own parents—no more than that—should be permitted. The Jesuit fathers thought it should, but priests of other orders convinced Pope Clement XI that it was contradictory to the Christian tenet of worshipping one God only. Ancestral worship was forbidden. The Pope could not possibly know that, as far as kneeling was concerned, the Chinese people always knelt on New Year's Day before their living parents *as human beings* and not as gods. The Pope should not have been surprised by the belief that human spirits are immortal and therefore continue to live after death. The Confucian dictum about filial piety is that " we should serve our parents when dead as we did when they were living "—by living a life worthy of their name. Emperor Kangshi decided he could not conscientiously repudiate ancestor worship. This would have endangered the sacred institution of the Taimiao (worship of the Imperial House), and have threatened the peace of his empire. Whatever fine theological points may have been involved, it implied in practice that Chinese Christians should learn to forget their gratitude to their parents and grandparents and cut themselves off from their own clan.

95. Large metal plate enamelled in the cloisonné technique; early seventeenth century.

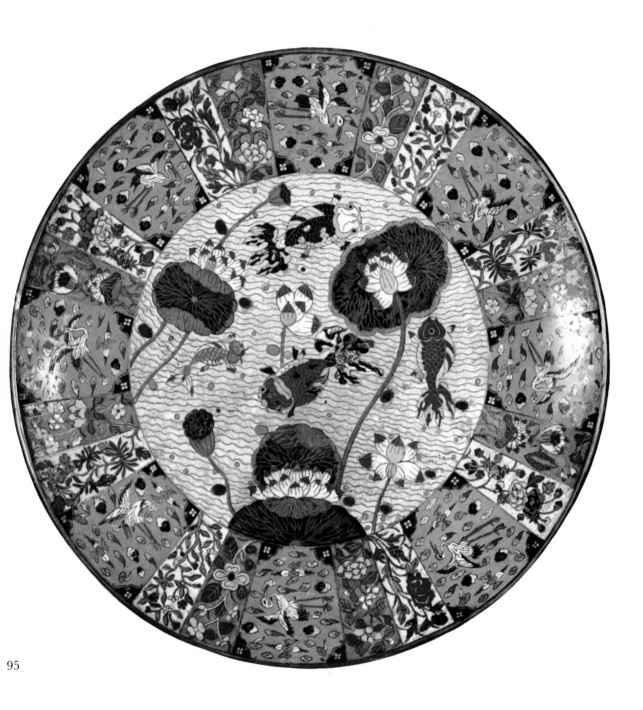

95

Adam Schall and Father Verbiest were skilled astronomers and mathematicians and they helped to correct the Chinese calendar. They were also charged to make maps of the country. Emperor Yungcheng (A. D. 1723-1735) disliked the missionaries, partly because they were involved in court politics concerning his fratricidal acts. The successor to Yungcheng, Emperor Chienlung (1735-1796), was again favourable to the Jesuits. Under his reign Father Benoist was charged with designing the Italian Palaces in the Old Summer Palace (Yuanmingyuan). At this time, Emperor Chienlung was in communication with Louis XV and they exchanged many presents, including silks, clocks, golden chalices and Gobelins. It is told that Emperor Chienlung, through a Father Amiot, also corresponded with Voltaire. One of the remarkable paintings in the Palace Museum is the painting of a " Hundred Horses " by Father Castiglione, who was known to the Chinese as Lang Shih-ning. Castiglione also painted Chienlung's portrait.

Two notable sites remain today to bear witness to the Jesuit influence. One is the Observatory built near the Eastern Wall on the southeast corner of the Inner City. The astronomical instruments it contains were made of bronze and supported by dragons of great beauty. Captured by the German Kaiser in 1900, they were returned to China after 1918, and have always attracted tourists by their fine workmanship. Another remarkable site is the Peitang, which means the " North Church," distinguished from the Nantang or South Church built directly inside the Shunchymen Gate on the site of Matteo Ricci's house. The Peitang has been destroyed twice, once by Yungcheng, and once during the Boxer Uprising, when some 400 Chinese Christian refugees died on this spot. On this occasion, thanks to the heroic leadership of Father Favier, a great many sisters and friars survived. It is remarkable that this Christian church was built right inside the Imperial City, an indication of the friendly attitude of Emperor Kangshi's household. It had an iron grille, presented by Louis XV. Towards the end of the nineteenth century, when it was restored, it passed into the hands of a Lazarist mission.

A story concerning a lion in the Zoological gardens of Paris shows how small the world had become by this time. During the siege of Paris in 1870, the people of Paris were reduced to eating the animals in their zoo. Father David of the Peitang, who was then in Paris, obtained permission to have the skin of a lion preserved for his collection in Peking. When the French troops arrived to relieve Peitang during the Boxer Uprising, they found this same lion who had seen the siege of Paris thirty years before.

96. Cloisonné animal: Chienlung period.

THE ART OF PEKING

by Peter C. Swann

FOR THE CASUAL visitor to Peking the city represents all that is China—the administrative centre of a huge country, the essence of a great culture stretching back about 4,500 years, the culmination of the world's longest unbroken tradition, the visual symbol of oriental splendour.

However, for the student of Chinese history, Peking tells only part of a long story, for it has been the capital of the nation during only a fraction of the time in which Chinese culture was born and flowered. And certainly nobody would claim that the period of Peking's greatness, the centuries covered by the Ming and Ch'ing dynasties—from 1368 to 1911—though notable, were in most respects the greatest periods of Chinese art and culture.

What is more, in considering Chinese art in general, it must not be forgotten thet during the last 2,000 years the nomadic peoples, "foreigners," have controlled all or part of China for nearly half the time. The invasions from the north drove the more conservative Chinese increasingly into the safer areas of the south where they fiercely and, on the whole, successfully guarded their ancient values. The north became the melting-pot for Chinese and nomadic blood—a process which enriched China as much as similar forced fusions have enriched other cultures.

These nomads, whom the Chinese always professed to despise and certainly feared, influenced Chinese life and art from at least 1000 B. C. Among other things they were responsible, if not for the introduction, at least for securely establishing Buddhism, which through them became a national religion and inspired some of the greatest works of Chinese art.

Chinese Buddhist art started by imitating the works made in the religious oases in Central Asia through which the faith made its way to China. Later, as communications improved, the Chinese were able to make direct contact with India and learn from its powerful sculptural traditions. However, strong as these were, the Chinese rapidly asserted their own personality on Buddhist art and thought. When in the Sung dynasty China was cut off from India and Buddhism was being wiped out in the country of its birth, the Chinese were able to develop new and indigenous forms. Illustrations 68 and 70, Yüan period Kuan-yin statues, show the final culmination of the sinicisation of monumental Buddhist sculpture. Although the Yüan and Ming dynasties produced little large sculpure of value (*ill.* 27 and 28), the modelling techniques were carried to perfection in the *blanc-de-Chine* figures of Fukien and these skills were continued in the Ch'ing period. (*Ill.* 105, 109, 110.) The elegant Kuan-yin

or " Goddess of Compassion " (*ill.* 105) shows the complete change of what was
an Indian masculine god into a delightful Chinese female goddess.

The freely executed " splashed ink " painting of an immortal in *ill.* 62 owes
much to yet another Chinese development of Buddhism—the Ch'an (better known
from the Japanese as *Zen*) form.   Its adherents believed that enlightenment must
come in a sudden flash and that painting done under its influence should express
itself in free, furious brushwork intended to express as far as possible the immediate nature of the inspiration.   The seeds of this unnaturalistic style of painting
had been sown in the T'ang Dynasty and their flowering in the Sung period added
tremendously to the range of Chinese art.   Without it much of the ink painting,
which seems so vital and modern to us, would not have been possible.[28]

The nomads, when they were successful, forced the Chinese to reassess their
achievements.   Thus in the 13th century, during the domination of the Mongols,
their barbarities led a few men of artistic genius to retire to the country where
they formulated principles of Chinese landscape painting which have lasted to
the present day.   One of the most famous was Ni Tsan, a landscape painter of
austere genius depicted in a portrait attributed to a Yüan dynasty painter (*ill.*
69).   The screen behind him is an echo of his style.   The foreigners, driven to
invade by envy and the urge to despoil, in their turn soon learned to appreciate
the value of the achievements of those they had conquered.   Generally they
became more Chinese than the Chinese themselves.   With the sole exception of
the Mongols, the Northerners jealously guarded Chinese culture, though often in
its more conservative aspects.   In doing so, they sometimes stimulated a reaction
which revived Chinese art.   The nomads chose Peking for their capital because
they felt basically insecure and needed an easy means of quick retreat to their
traditional homelands just outside the Great Wall.   Again and again they were
driven back to them.

To the art lover Peking means also the Palace Museum—which, as one might
expect, contains one of the greatest collections of Chinese art, especially painting.   One should perhaps say that there are now two Palace Museums—the one
which the fleeing nationalists carried with them to Formosa and which included
the finest collection of paintings in the world, and the second Palace Museum
which the communist régime is building up from what the nationalists could not
remove and from the fruits of the extensive archaeological research which it
encourages.

As a public museum, it is a relatively young institution—the creation of Yüan
Shih-k'ai who in 1912 became the second President of the Provisional Government of the Republic.   Yüan, to everybody's surprise, threw open part of the
Forbidden City, which had been closed for centuries—and this despite his not
so secret ambitions to assume " the Mandate of Heaven " and become the founder
Emperor of a new dynasty.   Popular opposition to the scheme and his own death
in 1916 thwarted these ambitions, but the Palace Museum rapidly became a
national institution.

That it contained such a wealth of material was due to another great Chinese
tradition associated with the ruling houses of China—Imperial patronage of the
arts.   Throughout history, few nations can compare with the Chinese in the
encouragement and support which their rulers have given to the arts and crafts.
As far back as the Shang dynasty (1523-1028 B. C.) in the bronze age, the crafts-
men who made the awesome ritual bronzes served the kings almost exclusively
and we know what tremendous prestige was attached to these vessels.   Like the
western crown, orb, sceptre and seals, the bronzes were often the symbols of power
as well as of wealth.

As in Europe in the 13th century the Christian religion, backed by the heads of Church and State, created the soaring Gothic cathedrals, so likewise in China the Buddhist faith in alliance with Imperial power in the 5th and 6th centuries created the monumental cave temples which, with their myriad sculptures carved out of the living rock, are among the artistic wonders of the world. The Emperors who backed these vast projects were originally nomads and certainly they felt that the Buddha, an alien god, was for them a deity preferable to those of China itself.[29] However, the Chinese also adopted the faith. The cave temples and their carvings overwhelm a man with their size and complexity—greater by far than anything mortal. Echoes continued into the Ming and Ch'ing dynasties, as can be seen in a representation of the Thousand Buddhas in the Winter Palace (ill. 1). By Ming times the great age of Buddhist sculpture was over. There remained capable repetitions of Sung models in the Yüan Dynasty wooden figures of Kuan-yin (ill. 68 and 70), and the more unusual Ming lacquer Buddha in Meditation of ill. 67.

The cave temples were only one aspect of Imperial patronage. During the T'ang Dynasty (618-907) the Emperors of China gathered around themselves at court the most notable painters in the land—supported and rewarded them often with the highest honours. The histories abound with stories of painting competitions and anecdotes concerning painters and their Imperial patrons.

Han Kan, to whom is attributed the study of two horses and their groom in ill. 37, was one of the favoured court painters of his day. He served Emperor Ming Huang at the full height of T'ang Dynasty power. The search for realistic expression was one of the fundamental directions of T'ang art as is seen from its tomb figures. The restrained vitality of these two horses is repeated in many a handsome tomb horse. The sense of movement which they so admirably convey is a key to the understanding of Chinese painting.

The T'ang Dynasty was equally renowned for its figure paintings and from the little that remains, the claim was not extravagant. Ill. 44 and 45, though later than T'ang, give an idea of typical court elegance of China in the 8th century. " The Palace Concert " (ill. 44) is a most skilled composition in which every figure has its variety and interest. In this period also landscape painting became firmly established as a major department of painting. Ill. 57, which may be an original of the 8th century or a later copy of about the 11th century, is in the " blue and green " style of the T'ang—a style which went out of fashion as the ink landscape painting became increasingly popular. Nevertheless it had its followers and copyists (see Ch'iu Ying's landscape in ill. 75) and it greatly influenced Japanese painting.

In times of internal disruption—as during the short interregnum between the fall of the T'ang in 907 and the rise of the Sung in 960—a period known as the Five Dynasties—many painters fled to the country to escape the dangers of politics and public service, there to commune with nature and to devote themselves to the development of their art.

Not a great deal has survived from this period. Ill. 39, a detail of " Deer in an Autumn Forest " by an anonymous artist, is both rare and untypical of Chinese landscape painting but it admirably conveys the spirit of communion with nature at which the Chinese always aimed. It also shows the fondness of Chinese artists for studying at first hand animal forms in all their variety. Is one not tempted to feel that perhaps the artist, himself a fugitive from the dangers of court life, felt an immediate sympathy for the hunted deer? The Chinese love of animals in art owes much to the nomads, for it completely dominates their art. The Chinese learned it from them and made it their own. It became a favourite theme for court painters in the refined form of bird and flower painting—the type of decorative painting which came to Europe and obscured the finer

97. Carved red lacquer brushholder: late Ming.

98. Carved red lacquer two-tiered box; Chienlung.

99. Jade sceptre (ju-i); eighteenth century. Length 13³/₄".

100. Imperial white jade seal of the Emperor Chienlung. 5" square.

101. White jade hat-stand; Chienlung period. Height 11".

97

98

creations of the art. *Ill.* 38 is of a typical court painting of birds and flowers and *ill.* 49, though in fact a textile, illustrates the grandeur to which this style can aspire. The Mongols of the Yüan Dynasty (1260-1368) managed to find some Chinese civil servants to work for them—and also a few painters such as the famous painter and calligrapher Chao Mêng-fu (1254-1322) whose " Sheep and Goat " (*ill.* 84) is among his few surviving works. I must confess not to be attracted to the sheep in this composition, but the goat has all the qualities of careful observation and fine draughtsmanship of Chinese animal painting. One of Chao's pupils, Jên Jên-fa, painted the kind of horse painting which the Mongols would have appreciated. His " Feeding Horses " in *ill.* 50 is splendidly atmospheric, and as fine a horse painting as ever produced in China.

Many Emperors were gifted poets, calligraphers and painters. The most famous, of course, was Hui Tsung of the Sung dynasty (reigned A. D. 1101-1125) under whom the academy flourished as never before. The Ming emperors scorned the politically weak Sung whom they held responsible for the Mongol invasion, but some of their emperors continued the artistic tradition and Hsüan-têh (1426-35) was a competent artist (*ill.* 79). In times of peace and prosperity aspiring painters would flock to the capital where they hoped to reap the rewards of court service. Sometimes the atmosphere of the court and the liberality of an educated Emperor stimulated great painting—sometimes an Emperor had fixed ideas as to what an artist should paint and how he should paint it, with unfortunate results. For then court art tended to become sterile and the most creative talents sought artistic freedom outside the favoured circle. Some, like Tai Chin (active early 15th century) who painted " Return from a Stroll in Early Spring " (*ill.* 73) started in the court but for some reason or other subsequently left it to work independently and died impoverished. His work here owes much to the Ma Yüan school but is essentially Ming in its interest in human detail and its elaboration of landscape details.

Despite the strictures of later writers, the court painters, especially during the Sung period, contributed very much to the Chinese art of painting. Two of the greatest Sung masters, Ma Yüan and Hsia Kuei—the founders of the " Ma-Hsia School " as it was called—created a style which became famous throughout the east and later throughout the west. Both were said to have learned much from Li T'ang, who is said to have painted the famous but untypical " Village Doctor " in *ill.* 66, but who was more famed for his misty landscapes which concentrate the attention on the foreground and then lead the eye to a few peaks which fade away in the far distance.

Ma Yüan used a diagonal composition, leaving one corner empty—" One Corner Ma " he was called. He produced romantic, soft, intimate landscapes in which man rather than nature is the dominant (*ill.* 51). All is peace and poetic emotion. Attractive though it certainly is, stripped of its oriental charm, is it not also a little whimsical? Hsia Kuei uses the same brushwork and ink washes to produce a far more powerful river landscape (*ill.* 52). *Ill.* 47, " Listening to the Wind in the Pines " by Ma Yüan's son Ma Lin, shows how very much this distinctive style was a family affair—and how open it was to debility!

Strangely enough to western understanding, the civil service, scholarship and the art of painting became over the centuries inextricably combined. As early as the Han Dynasty (206 B. C.-A. D. 221) the Chinese laid the foundations of their civil service system—one of the corner-stones of Chinese civilisation. Entrance to it was by examination open to all ranks of life. Poverty was no bar to the ambitious student. Fortunate was the young man who had succeeded in the local examinations and who then went to the national tests in the capital.

102. Copper-gilt brushholder in the form of an ox, with champlevé and cloisonné enamel. Inscribed ' Chien-lung Fang-ku ' (Chienlung period imitating the antique). Height 7 1/2 ", length 8".

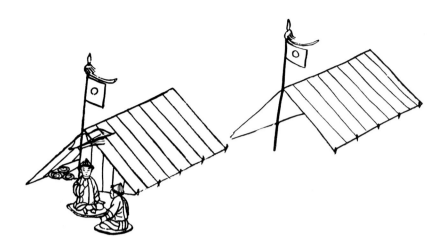

If then, in the competition with the best brains in the land, he passed top of the lists he paraded through the city on horseback and his future was assured. Ministers sought his friendship and offered him their daughters in marriage!

With the development of this system of administration of a huge empire there also grew up the custom for scholar-officials to seek their relaxation in the pursuit of the arts, especially those of painting and calligraphy. There were always professional painters at court academies but they fell into increasing disrepute over the centuries as the scholar-painter, the " man of letters," the *wên-jên* began to dominate the field. Through their writings they secured the triumph of their theories that painting should be exclusively the spiritual refuge of the non-professional. For them painting and calligraphy must remain the other-worldly pursuits of men of culture, pure expressions of the spirit untouched by taint of financial considerations. The painter hero was the man who painted only when the spirit moved him, who suffered poverty for his art, who gave away his paintings to those whom he thought understood and appreciated them, who turned away the man who came to his door with a bag of gold to buy his creations. The idea was a noble one, though open to the danger of artistic sterility. However, on the whole, it influenced generation upon generation of scholar-painters —especially those in secure positions—it inspired them to study the arts and often to practise them most skilfully—but in fact it never worked to the complete exclusion of the talented artist out of official employment who was forced, however thinly, to disguise his professionalism. Surely no country has ever produced such a " civilised " civil service. The court provided the battlefield for the professional and non-professional painters. The latter won, for they were the articulate critics and historians and accordingly the professionals suffered in the eyes of history. Only now can we assess the achievements of the professional painters more fairly. Ch'ên Hung-shou (1599-1652), who served the Ming court in its final days at Nanking, was a landscapist and also a bird and flower painter of originality and genius. The painting in *ill.* 87 belongs to the painting category of Birds and Flowers but is far removed from the " Partridge and Sparrow " attributed to Huang Chutsai (*ill.* 38) of the 10th century and the silk picture " Birds and Flowers " (*ill.* 60). In its final development this type of painting was to become familiar to the world from the decoration of Ch'ing dynasty *famille verte* and *famille rose* porcelain (*ill.* 107 and 108).

Calligraphy was always considered as much an art as painting; it has in fact been called the basis of all Chinese art, " a national taste, a common aesthetic instinct nourished in every Chinese from childhood up." [30] Examples by past

masters were revered and their styles and brushwork closely studied. A good hand was essential for a cultivated man and for entry into the civil service. To the Chinese a man's writing expresses his character in a singularly direct manner. Chiang Yee, who has written one of the few books in a western language on this esoteric art, judges Su Tung-p'o's character from his hand as follows: " The writing of Su Tung-p'o suggests for me a man fatter, shorter, more careless in nature than Mi Fei, but broad-minded, vigorous, a great laughter-maker and a great laugher." [31] We reproduce a piece of Su Tung-p'o's calligraphy in *ill.* 65. Poet, painter, calligrapher and cultivated man of letters, in many ways his life epitomizes the refined spirit of Sung times.[32] His brush shows how this is the purest form of abstract art, a successful composition which has harmony and balance, inner tension, pleasant rhythms, complete assurance allied with a fluent and faultless technique, vitality, spontaneity—a living quality which is unknown to western writing.

From calligraphy it is a comparatively short step to the painting of bamboo (*ill.* 85) which has always been one of the most testing subjects of Chinese painting. Some artists spent their lives in trying to depict this plant in its many moods and species. Anybody who finds beauty in the curves and straight lines of calligraphy will immediately understand the fascination of bamboo painting.

No rivalry between professional and non-professional existed in the crafts. Craftsmen were always humble professionals. From T'ang times onwards the emperors established ateliers near or even within the court to provide fine objects for Imperial use. The finest Sung ceramics for example, were made in Imperial kilns, though some of the output always reached people outside the palace. The Ming Emperors needed colourful tiles like the dragon in *ill.* 17, porcelains, cloisonné and lacquer to match the flamboyant architecture of newly built Peking and even to bury with them, as the newly discovered tomb of Emperor Wan-li (1573-1619) has disclosed (*ill.* 81 and 82). The Manchus followed the example of the Ming and established some 27 workshops within the palace precincts for metalwork, cloisonné, jade, gold, ivory carving, lacquer manufacture, jewel-mounting and many other crafts—even one exclusively for the manufacture of jade *ju-i* sceptres (*ill.* 99).

The painting which the Manchu Emperors actively supported was the traditional type, codified during the Ming and stabilised by scholars like Tung Ch'i-ch'ang. Although very accomplished, it had by now become somewhat stereotyped and debilitated. The more progressive spirits then, as always in the past, remained well outside the privileges—and bonds—of Imperial patronage. Such a revolutionary was Shih-tao, a descendant of the Ming imperial house who found political security from the dangers of early Ch'ing times in a Buddhist hermit-like life. One of the leading individualists, he refused to allow the old masters to hamstring his imagination and his highly personal work is among the most prized of all late Chinese painting (*ill.* 118 and 119).

Among the few innovators whom the Manchu Emperors tolerated were the Jesuit priest painters who for a while dazzled the court with their unfamiliar naturalism—with scientific perspective, chiaroscuro and with the truth to life of their portraits. Ch'ien-lung was flattered to have Castiglione, known as Lang Shih-ning to his Chinese colleagues, accompany him on his expeditions and record for posterity such scenes of imperial power as when the Kirghizes presented him with tribute horses (*ill.* 20). Sometimes a Chinese artist would collaborate with Castiglione and paint the landscape backgrounds for his figures.

The study of Chinese painting is still in its infancy. It is made still more difficult by the output of such artists as Ch'iu Ying who was active in the first half of the 16th century. He was not a court painter, nor did he belong to the group of scholar-poet-calligraphers who were beginning to dominate the field. The biographies and Chinese records tell us little about him. He came of humble origins and was simply a very able painter who had fully assimilated a number of past styles or elements from them. Often he copied ancient paintings, as in *ill.* 74 and 75, his aim being as he said to " hold up antiquity as a mirror to his own time." Sirén says of some of Ch'iu Ying's paintings " the fact that they have become so famous all over the world and sometimes been hailed as supreme examples of Ming painting, is no doubt to be found in their illustrative appeal combined with their decorative beauty and refinement of execution." [33] He thinks that a group or atelier may have been responsible for some of Ch'iu Ying's many paintings, though in the present state of our knowledge this seems difficult to determine. His work in the " blue and green " style goes back to the landscapes of the T'ang dynasty, to such works as " The Emperor Ming Huang's Journey to Shu," a detail of which is reproduced in *ill.* 57.

Certainly we owe a great deal of our knowledge of early painting styles to the accomplished copies he made of them. One says copies, but indeed they have too much life and atmosphere to be merely dead copies. And he could paint in a completely convincing landscape style which could only be of his time. The detail of a large landscape " Waiting for the Ferry in Autumn " in *ill.* 89 is neither artificial (the trademark of the court painter) nor dead (that of the dry copyist). It is full of sympathetic love of nature and of that desire to be at one with nature which inspires all the greatest Chinese landscape artists. The Chinese—intensely traditional—admire individuality but they also demand that an artist understands his past inheritance. They like to be able to recognize something from the past in a man's work, no matter how it may have been transformed. A dot or a line, a rock or a tree invented by an ancient artist and suggested by a later painter, created an immediate bond of common cultural traditions as would a few words of a Latin tag to a 19th century European.

China has made many contributions to the culture of humankind, but none has served man better than their invention of porcelain. From the earliest times the Chinese showed natural gifts for the craft. Even the neolithic painted pottery of the third millennium B. C. is far more skilled in technique and decoration than that produced by other cultures at a similar stage in their development.

103. ' Eight Saints ':
anonymous
eighteenth century painter.

103

The highly-fired white stoneware of the Shang Dynasty has a refinement of technique which anticipates the invention of porcelain by about two thousand years. For a few centuries after the Shang dynasty the Chinese seem to have abandoned their interest in developing ceramics. Simple pottery for household use was always made but it was not until about the third century B. C. that they invented a ware known from the place of its manufacture as Yüeh. This, after a long period of development and refinement which lasted about a thousand years, finally led to the invention of porcelain.

The T'ang dynasty was renowned for its pottery—especially the tomb figures in which the life of the 7th and 9th centuries is so vividly portrayed. The Lohan or Disciple of the Buddha in *ill.* 63 was not made during the T'ang dynasty but during the northern Liao or Chin dynasty which in pottery closely followed T'ang traditions. The Liao Dynasty was established in the north by the Khitans, a nomadic people. From 1004 their empire included parts of China. It fell before yet another nomadic invasion, that of the Chins in 1124, which in its turn fell to the Mongols. Like the Northern Wei before them, both nomadic tribes rapidly adopted Chinese culture and their admiration for it led them to preserve into the tenth-thirteenth centuries some of the typical art forms of the T'ang period.

Once the Chinese had discovered the full secrets of porcelain manufacture, their creations were unsurpassed. The wares of the Sung dynasty are considered by most experts to be the finest creations of a universal craft. It took the west many centuries to learn the secrets of the Chinese. Sung wares included a creamy white ware known as *ting*, a very pale blue known as *Ching-pai*, the lavender *ju*, the rarest of all, and a humble but very vigorous type with black painting on white slip or incised decoration known as *tzu-chou*. One of the most beautiful of the Sung wares was a type known as *kuan* or " official " ware, much of which was intended to serve the exclusive use of the palace. Crackle in porcelain generally occurs as a result of the glaze and body having different coefficients of expansion. The Chinese developed what was originally an accident into a means of decoration of great variety and subtlety. The use of crackle became a criterion of the potter's skill in the handling of his material. Both pieces in *ill.* 53 and 54 once belonged to the Imperial Collection and both show the subtle variety which could be achieved in crackle. The vase in *ill.* 53, now in the Percival David Collection, has a poem inscribed on the inside by Emperor Ch'ien-lung. His appreciation is in agreement with one of our most distinguished modern connoisseurs, who stated recently that in his opinion " for sheer technical achievement these *kuan* wares stand head and shoulders above the other Sung Wares." [34] So great was the Imperial appreciation of this ware that the potters were ordered to imitate it and some very fine pieces were produced in the 18th century. Some of these 18th century copies carry dates, but some do not and there is a suspicion that some pieces in our collections with Sung labels may in fact be 18th century copies.

Kuan was only one of a number of types of porcelain and stoneware produced by the Sung potters. Some of them were continued in the following Mongol and Ming dynasties. The Mongols at one time intended to wipe out Chinese civilisation and turn the land into pasture for their herds. Fortunately they saw the advantage of keeping Chinese civilisation intact and at their service. Thus many branches of Chinese art were able to develop without too great damage. The celadon dish in *ill.* 59 follows in direct succession from the celadons of the Sung period and was produced either in the Yüan or Early Ming period. As a type, celadon wares have been called the " backbone " of oriental ceramics and their history goes back to at least the third century B. C. In the Sung

104. A ' peach bloom ' vase. This was a much prized glaze colour produced from copper, and introduced by a superintendent of the Imperial Kiln during the reign of Kangshi (1662-1722).

189

they were brought to perfection and many of the Ming examples, though less subtle in colour, have a splendid power of drawing and modelling.

The black jar in *ill.* 58 again descends from the Sung type known as *tzu-chou.* The two bold Chinese characters in white relief, " nei-fu ", mean " Inner Palace." The same two characters start a longer inscription on the wine jar covered with crackled turquoise glaze (*ill.* 80) where the four characters " nei-fu kung yung " mean " offered for use in the Inner Palace." Early in the 15th century the Chinese emperors established an Imperial factory at Ching-tê Chên and from this time onwards the taste of the court influenced profoundly the quality and taste of the finest pieces. The fortunes of the Imperial kilns varied throughout the Ming centuries but many provincial kilns also provided a wealth of admirable ceramic wares. A large part of Ming ceramic production was in blue-and-white, and lively but somewhat coarse examples produced for export are found in places as far distant as the Oxus Valley and in many parts of the African continent, to say nothing of the Imperial pieces presented to the monarchs of the Middle East.[35] In time the export wares reached Europe literally in their tens of thousands. *Ill.* 90 and 91 show examples of early blue-and-white. Both are of finest quality; the flask shaped jar dates from the second half of the 14th century. The earliest period of which we have examples is the early 14th century and although these are painted with great freedom, they are comparatively crude in technique. The late 14th century pieces have a vigour of colour and decoration which is quite distinctive. By the Hsüan-têh period (1426-35) when the jar in *ill.* 91 was manufac-tured, the process of technical refinement had progressed considerably and the Imperial kilns set up just a little before were turning out skilled works which were the envy of the world. We can trace the progress of blue-and-white, the development of styles, the refinement of techniques, throughout the 15th, 16th, 17th and 18th century. By the time of the Manchu Emperor K'ang-hsi the Imperial potteries were again manufacturing to satisfy the most fastidious taste. The K'ang-hsi wares with their pure white background and deep, almost lumi-nous blue decoration reached a degree of technical perfection which had never before been achieved. Mass production methods were employed. *Ill.* 114 shows a vase with decoration of prunus on a blue background suggesting cracking ice —the symbol of springtime. This decoration, often found on ginger jars, persists down to the present day, when degraded examples are still employed for exporting ginger to the west. Here the drawing and colours are of masterly assurance. The same design is found on the pink background bowl in *ill.* 113, although this is made not of porcelain but of Canton enamel.

The *famille verte* vase is of the type which displaced blue-and-white in European favour towards the end of the 18th and in the 19th centuries. The type was a development of the Ming dynasty *wu-ts'ai* or " five coloured " over-glaze enamelled painting but here substituting under-glaze blue for the Ming turquoise. The variety in this type of ware is inexhaustible and the Chinese decorators called on the vast range of Chinese symbolism, folklore, myth and indeed also upon the extensive figure painting repertoire of late Ming and early Ch'ing times. The birds and flowers which had occupied Chinese artists for centuries were also pressed into service, as can be seen in *ill.* 108. This fine " moon " flask belongs to the *famille rose* group of wares which began in the late Kang-hsi period. They take their name from the pink enamel which was introduced into China from Europe. This was what the Chinese know as the " foreign colour " and they used it to great advantage. Many plates of the shape and design of that in *ill.* 117 were produced in *famille rose* colouring and as here on eggshell porcelain of featherweight. This example, however, is more unusual in that black and red enamels and gilt were used for the designs. Here technique seems to have run

105. A figure of Kuan-yin in *blanc-de-chine* porcelain; an excellent example of eighteenth century modelling by Fukien potters.

190

away with taste. I know of no other art work in which refinement is carried to quite such a degree.

Many of the late porcelains with their purity of colour and exquisite drawing are undoubtedly the world's most technically accomplished ceramic wares. The rarest of all are the Ku Yüeh Hsüan type wares illustrated in *ill.* 107. Its finest examples were made when the famous director of the Imperial Porcelain Factory T'ang Yin was in charge—between 1727-1753. It ceased when T'ang Yin died in 1754.[36] Some authorities believe that Castiglione, the Jesuit painter, who so impressed the court of Ch'ien-lung, influenced the artists of this Imperial ware even if he did not actually paint some of them himself. The plate has a poem which has been rendered in English as " Moving shadows follow the round moon, The gentle breeze bears fragrance." The two small bottles have the lines " Dew is fragrant in the middle of autumn " and " Elegance the autumnal branches reveal, Wonderful are the blossoms in their various hues."

The monochrome or self-colour porcelains of the Ming and Ch'ing dynasties must have been responsible for more people becoming addicts of Chinese wares than any other group. Their colours are of unsurpassed purity and range from delicate lavender to powerful ox-blood, from imperial yellow to bright apple-green, from mirror black to peach bloom. The shapes are almost invariably severely classical—allowing the colours and the perfection of the glazes to speak for themselves. The small vase in *ill.* 104 of peach-bloom hue belongs to the rarest group and is in the colour which even the Chinese potters found most difficult to control. This is porcelain at its zenith of perfection.

Yet another group of wares which early attracted western admiration (and imitation) was the *blanc-de-chine, tê-hua* as it is called in China, of Fukien province. Starting in the 15th century its finest flowering was from about 1600 to 1750, the period in which the figures of *ill.* 105, 109 and 110 were made. It is interesting to see that, even when monumental Buddhist sculpture declined, Chinese sculptural talents survived and were directed into these smaller works in porcelain. Here we have two very different versions of Bodhidharma, the teacher who is credited with being the first to introduce Ch'an (Zen) Buddhism into China. The skill of the Fukien workmen in depicting draperies is here well illustrated—as it is also in *ill.* 105, where the supremely peaceful Kuan-yin, " Goddess of Compassion, " leans gracefully to balance the swirl of her robes. In such fine pieces the modellers seem to have frozen the movements of an un-felt breeze as if in the purest ice. We have few criteria for judging the date of these wares very closely—a creamy glaze is supposed to be an indication of Ming rather than Ch'ing date, but this is by no means a certain test. The *blanc-de-chine* tradition was strong and has lasted down even to the present day when passable echoes of former masterpieces reach us from the mainland through the outlet of Hongkong. Whatever demands an export drive may place on modern potters they are unlikely to try to repeat the technical *tour-de-force* in *blanc-de-chine* reproduced in *ill.* 116—a small openwork bowl of incredible potter's skill.

However, no material so completely tests and demonstrates the Chinese crafts-men's skill as jade. Jade, of course, is found in Maori and in pre-Columbian American civilisations but it particularly distinguishes Chinese culture from the very earliest times. We know that the stone-age people treasured it and from the Shang period onwards the material has been considered as something very precious. A whole symbolism has grown up round jade—it is equated with purity and steadfastness—its colours, sound, texture, hardness, all, to the Chinese, have a significance. Jade seems to have been used at all periods but as yet dating of it has been very much a hazardous undertaking. With the increase of controlled excavations, it may be possible to obtain a few clues to the age

106. Vase and cover in pale green jade; eighteenth century. Height 10³/₄".

of many of the perplexing pieces in our collections. Pieces made prior to 900 B. C. are fairly easy to identify but after that, as Hansford remarks, " we enter a desert, in which landmarks are rare and mirages plentiful and seductive." [37] Such objects as the jade bowl in *ill.* 81, from the tomb of Emperor Wan-li of the Ming (r. 1573-1619), are rare and this one is so classical in shape that it tells us little. Most of the early jade came from Central Asia and must have been costly. Thus it is not surprising to find so many of the finest pieces connected in some way with the palace and the various emperors. The jade sceptre (*ju-i*) (*ill.* 99) and the strange mushroom-like hat-stand (*ill.* 101) are typical of the finest work of the Imperial workshops of emperor Ch'ien-lung. The pure white jade of these is the most highly-prized. The seal in *ill.* 100 would have been used to affix the royal seal on documents—and unfortunately sometimes also on paintings, thereby disfiguring them. The manufacture of seals of jade, usually reserved for emperors, must have taxed the skill of the carvers to the utmost. More grandiose is the jade vase and cover of *ill.* 106, vaguely reminiscent of an archaic bronze form and of a rare smoky green colour. It is pierced and incised to the highest standards of workmanship. No metal is hard enough to cut jade and the carvers used abrasive sands and fairly simple rotary tools. The results obtained from such comparatively primitive methods are masterpieces of delicate craftsmanship.

Lacquer work also is a distinguishing characteristic of far eastern civilisations, particularly of the Chinese and subsequently of the Japanese, who learned it from China. It was manufactured as early as the Chou centuries. The resinous product of the lacquer tree is purified and painted on to a wooden or hemp

107. A group of Ku-yueh Hsuan style porcellains; early Chienlung period.

108. 'Moon' flask decorated in *famille rose* colours; made in the reign of Yung-cheng (1723-35). Height 11½".

109. *The-hua* (*blanc-de-chine*) figure of Bodhidharma, 28th Indian patriarch of Buddhism, and reputed first patriarch of Buddhism of China; late Ming. Height 10¼".

110. *Te-hua* figure of Bodhidharma crossing the sea on a millet stalk, with one shoe in his hand, having left the other in his tomb; the Emperor, hearing of his re-appearance in the world, had the tomb opened and found there only the other shoe. Seventeenth century. Height 6½".

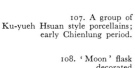

109 110

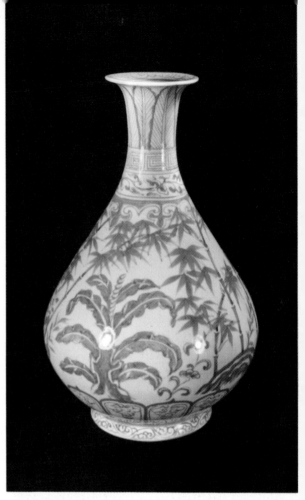

base. The clear liquid can be coloured—and by far the majority of Chinese pieces are of a characteristic " sealing wax " red, derived from cinnabar. Once sufficient coats have been applied, the material is thick enough to be carved and it is then that the inherent carving skill of the Chinese reveals itself in a thousand objects of great decorative beauty. Light and strong, it survives the centuries. From the Yüan dynasty onwards carved lacquer was made in many parts of China and much of it reached Peking to serve in the various palaces. The bottle in *ill.* 92, of late Ming date, has a favourite all-over peony pattern, while the brush-holder in *ill.* 97, of about the same period, transfers a court scene, familiar from painting, into the lacquer technique. *Ill.* 98, a two-tiered box of the mid-18th century, carries a charming detail of a lake landscape. The workmanship of this period is as fine as that of the earlier periods but the designs tend to become crowded, weaker and the whole effect can be one of over-elaborateness.

Of the other sumptuary art represented here, cloisonné, we know little. It was certainly introduced from the west. The Chinese know it as " Arabian ware " or by the Chinese word for Byzantium.[38] It seems probable that the technique was introduced into China by emigrating Islamic craftsmen, possibly as early as the Yüan period. Certainly by the beginning of the 15th century, pieces of outstanding quality were being made for the Ming court. These early pieces, which in their designs have strong affinities to early Ming blue-and-white wares, are perhaps the most attractive of all works in cloisonné but the workshops continued to manufacture large quantities with a high degree of craftsmanship throughout the following four centuries. The three pieces in *ill.* 95, 96 and 102 are all of the 17th and 18th centuries. The large plate in *ill.* 95 shows the 17th century increased interest in plants and animals, while the fierce animal of *ill.* 96 has, in its somewhat repulsive way, all the pomp and intimidating circumstance which one associates with the " Forbidden City." The wistful creature in *ill.* 102, worked in a combination of champlevé and cloisonné methods, illustrates the force of tradition in Chinese art for it looks back, perhaps somewhat sadly, to the very earliest days of Chinese culture—to the great period of the bronzes. The emperors in Peking, whether native or foreign, were always conscious of the past to which they were heirs. From their palaces in Peking and surrounded by the riches of Chinese art, they surveyed a land which they had conquered and which had conquered them.

111. Porcelain vase; Kangshi period. Height 13³/₄"; diameter 6³/₄".

112. Grey and white vase; Ming — Hung-wu period.

113. Pink Canton enamel bowl; Kangshi. Diameter 6".

114. Porcelain vase painted in underglaze blue; Kangshi. Height 17".

APPENDIX
Research on the History of Peking

I: Ming Period

An immense amount of painstaking research has been done to determine the relative sizes and sites of Peking in the different periods. The historically-minded Chinese have kept many records for such research. In the first place, the official histories of the successive dynasties always include a section devoted to geography, and records were kept of the measurements and building of the city walls and the exact names of the gates of the palaces and the city. Secondly come the *Fuchy*, or district histories. For Peking there is the *Shuntien Fuchy*, first compiled in 1593, revised in 1885, and also the *Shitsinchy*, compiled in the fourteenth century, which gives even the names of the streets and police precincts. Thirdly, the doings of the emperors, called *Shylu*, were scrupulously recorded; hunts, visits to the various parks, football or acrobatics—these are all included. The *Shylu* of the first emperor of the Ming Dynasty is an outstanding example. In the fourth place, for the Ming and Mongol periods, there was a special geographical work, the *Peiping Tuching Shuchy*, edited under the first Ming Emperor, Hungwu. Lastly, there exists the most popular form of literary composition, *pichi*, or notebooks.

The notebooks, as the name implies, contain entries of the most varied kinds, such as a story heard one evening that may have some significance, or an ancient inscription on a stone half-buried in the ground, noticed during an afternoon stroll. An anecdote may be followed by a poem, the description of a visit to some ancient site may follow a philosophic observation. The writer records it for what it is worth, and no arrangement is necessary. Some of them wrote down the current " literary gossip," while others recorded sidelights on historic events and were most careful about the accuracy of their facts.

115. *Famille verte* vase; Kangshi.

116. White porcelain bowl with open fretted sides, with a poetic description included in the fret; Ming Dynasty — Wan-li period (1573-1619). Diameter 3¹/₄".

117. Porcelain plate painted in black and red enamels and gilt; early Chienlung. Diameter 8³/₈".

All these available sources concerning Peking have been collated in the authoritative *Jyshia Chiuwen Kao* (see Chapter 4). There are two other modern sources since the *Jyshia*. One is the *Yenchingchi*, a summary of the historical events and vicissitudes of fortune of the city of Peking, written by Ku Yünsen in 1756, discovered in 1939 and published in the *Yenching Fengtu Tsungshu*. The other is a contemporary study on the subject, *Peiching Chienchy Tankwei*, by Chü Shüanying, published in *Peiching Lishy Fengtu Tsungshu*. It represents more or less the latest Chinese opinion on the subject.

For purposes of comparison in discussing and determining the sites of the

115 116
117

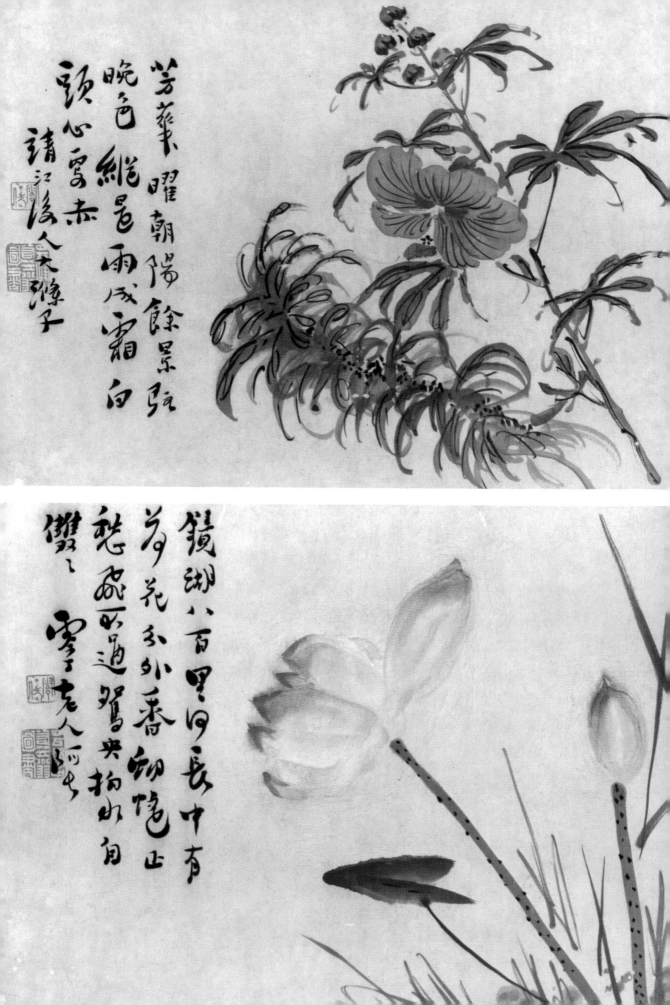

ancient capitals, it is necessary to know the exact size of the present city. Osvald Sirén has done a piece of scholarly, definitive work in his *Walls and Gates of Peking*. There he examines the construction of the city walls almost yard by yard. The most exact measurements were made in 1874 by two French naval officers, MM. Fleuriais and Lapied when they went to Peking to observe the passage of the planet Venus. According to their measurements, the Inner City has a circumference of 41.26 *li* (a *li* is 1,800 Chinese feet and 3 *li* are equivalent to 1.074 English miles). These measurements are given in *Péking, Histoire et Description* by Alphonse Pierre Favier (1837-1905), Apostolic Vicar of Peking, published by the Lazaristes at Pei-tang, 1897, and Lille, 1900. (Father Favier became celebrated during the siege of Peking in 1900. He used the semi-French spelling " Péking " on account of established association.) I have placed side by side Lapied's measurements and those given by the Section on Public Works (*Kungpuchy*) in the *Ming History* as quoted in *Jyshia Chiuwen Kao*, vol. 32, p. 12. The *Ming History* gives the measurements as those of the city built by Emperor Yunglo, that is, the present Inner City.

	Lapied	Ming History
South Wall:	11.64 li	7.2 li (12,959.4 Ch. ft.)
North Wall:	11.81 li	12.4 li (22,324.5 Ch. ft.)
East Wall:	9.27 li	9.9 li (17,869.3 Ch. ft.)
West Wall:	8.54 li	8.7 li (15,645.2 Ch. ft.)

The small difference in length between the East and West Walls and that between the North and South Walls are due to a slight bend in the northwest corner of the city.

Except in the measurements of the South Wall, the figures agree fairly closely. The figure given in feet by the Chinese record for the South Wall is obviously a misprint in the feet measurements, 12,000 being substituted for 22,000, as it is impossible that there should be such a vast difference between the south and the north wall. Such a mistake is easily made with Chinese characters. I have found another such mistake on the same page, 23 being given for 32, referring to the year of Chiatsing's reign when the Outer City was built. Lapied's measurements are accepted by Sirén, who says that the city is between 41 and 42 *li*. The discrepancy in the Chinese official measurements, due to the misprint mentioned, would bring the circumference down to 38.2 *li*. A correction of the misprint to make the South Wall 22,959 feet instead of 12,959 would make it approximately of the same length as the North Wall.

In the same passage from the *Ming History*, the measurements given for the walls of the Outer City are as follows:

South Wall:	24,544.7 Chinese ft.
East Wall:	18,151.0 Chinese ft.
West Wall:	19,132.0 Chinese ft.

The total given is 28 *li*.

The height of the walls of the Inner City is given as 35.5 feet and that of the parapet at 5.8 feet. Its width at the base is 62 feet, and at the top 50 feet. There is another obvious misprint in the figures for the height and width of the outer walls. Their width is given as 10 feet at the base, but 14 feet at the top. The figure for the base should obviously be 20 feet.

When the first Ming Emperor Hungwu overthrew the Mongol régime, he established his capital at Nanking. Yunglo was then the Prince of Yen, with his

118. 119. 'Flowers :
Tao Chi (1630-1707).
Two leaves
from a twelve-leaf album.

seat of power in Peking; he had no idea of succeeding to the throne. In time the empire passed to the grandson of Hungwu, the crown prince having died. This young man, Chienwen, was highly suspicious of his five uncles who were princes in different regions, and he started a campaign to take over their power. Yunglo saw one of his brothers captured and exiled, another burn himself to death, a third forcibly deposed and a fourth imprisoned at Tatung. He himself came under attack in the very first year of Chienwen's régime, and war continued for another three years. Several times he was almost defeated and once he almost lost his life. In 1402 he set out towards the south and captured Nanking. Chienwen fled, and vanished; a popular legend persists that he shaved his head and became a monk. Incidentally, Yunglo's reign was associated with the height of Chinese sea power when his fleet, 20,000 strong, sailed as far as Madagascar and compelled tribute from the Indonesian islands.

In July 1406, in the fourth year of Yunglo, plans for the rebuilding of the palaces and city walls began. Active rebuilding was done between 1417 and 1420, and on January 1, 1421, the new capital was declared completed. Whereas the Yüan city had been made of mud, strengthened with reeds and straw, the use of bricks and stone for the walls began with Yunglo. What is not so clear is the statement in the biography of Yunglo that in 1419, he also built or extended the south city by 27,000 feet, or 15 li. If this is correct, then the building of the south city must have begun in Yunglo's time.

A lesser known part of the story is the role which the Emperor Chengtung (A. D. 1436-1449) played in strengthening the city with stoneworks. He set about improving the fortifications with the aid of the army and made no levy of money or labour from the people. The strength and beauty of the city walls is due very largely to his effort. In 1439, he repaired and strengthened the gate towers, added many outer towers, and replaced the wooden bridges with stone ones. He deepened the moats and built banks of stone and bricks around them. Under the bridge leading into each gate, he set up water-gates for control, thus making the water flow round the city from the northwest corner to the southeast corner.

The next great work was done during the reign of the Emperor Chiatsing, who started building the present Outer City in 1553. A great settlement had grown up in the area south of Chienmen and it was thought unfair to leave the people in the suburbs unprotected in case of war. At first the idea had been to build an outer city on all sides, with a circumference of 70 li. However, Chiatsing was worried about the cost and asked the Prime Minister Yen Sung for his opinion. Yen Sung went out to the suburbs to examine the work required, and came back to report that in his opinion the Outer City should be completed on the south side first; the other three sides could be added when circumstances permitted. It was decided in council that, although it had been planned to build a south wall originally of 20 li, now since only the south side was to be built, 12 or 13 li should suffice. (The Inner City south wall was only about 10.5 li.) Accordingly it was decided to make a turn at points on the southeast and southwest, and to continue the lines northwards so as to join up with the south corners of the Inner City wall. This explains the awkward bulge at the south corners of the Outer City. The length of this Outer City of three sides was recorded as 28 li.

With this, the building of the city was virtually complete. The Ching (Manchu) emperors devoted themselves to renovating and beautifying the old structures. They changed neither the city limit itself, nor the names of the palaces, and only some of the names of the gates. The Mings had changed four of the gate names, but as always happens, the people still use the names given in Mongol times. This is especially true in the case of the Pingtsemen (officially Fuchengmen) on the west, the Chihuamen (officially Chaoyangmen), and the Hatamen (officially Tsungwenmen). The common rickshaw puller would be completely puzzled to be told to go to Tsungwenmen, and if you pointed it out to him he would say, " Why didn't you say Hatamen? " Hata was the name of a Mongol prince whose residence was near the gate. The exception is the Shunchymen, the west gate on the south wall, officially called the Shüanwumen, named after the first emperor of the Manchu Dynasty, Shunchy.

For the Mongol period, we fortunately have three detailed descriptions of the Mongol capital. These are: Tao Tsungyi's *Chuokenglu* (Records After Farming), Shiao Shün's *Kukung Yilu* (Visits to the Old Mongol Palaces), and *Peiping Tuching Chyshu* (Atlas of Peiping) compiled under Emperor Hungwu. Shiao Shün, when he was inspecting Peking as Secretary for Public Works, took the trouble to record in detail the palaces of the Mongol Dynasty after its overthrow. Tao Tsungyi (around 1360) made a detailed record of the city and the palaces. Tao, in particular, made a point of recording the exact measurements of the buildings which he visited. In addition, there are the official histories, *Yüanchy* and *Yüan Tungyi Chy*.

Kublai Khan had at first intended to build his new capital upon the site of the old Chin city, but decided to break fresh ground on its northeast where the present Peking lies. Doubtless he was attracted by the glazed roofs of the superb Chin summer palace and its pavilions, particularly the Moon Palace at the top where now stands the White Dagoba of Peihai. According to Chin records, these were known in Chin times as Chiunghuatao Island and Taiyichy Lake. He built his palaces on the east of the present Middle Sea and North Sea, and as both Marco Polo and Chinese sources tell us later added new palaces for his sons on their west. The whole of this area is now inside the so-called Imperial City, or Huangcheng.

Chinese authoritative opinion, that of the editors of *Jyshia Kao* for example, holds that the Yüan Palaces were centred more in the Three Seas area, and that when later the Ming Emperor Yunglo planned his palaces, the centre had shifted a little to the east. There was no exact record of how much it had shifted, but the editors, who had all the historical sources at their command, never suggested that the present east and west walls were not in the same position as the Mongol walls.

The confusion is partly caused by two old statements. First, Marco Polo stated that Kublai Khan's city had a circumference of 24 miles, 6 miles on each side. This was considered by Osvald Sirén and Emil Bretschneider as inaccurate and excessive. Secondly, Marco Polo stated that the Bell Tower was the centre of the city. Now the old Mongol Bell Tower was not on the north of the Drum Tower, as it is today, but close on its east, where Wanningsy is. Chinese records make this even more explicit; they mention the Chungshintai, or Centre Terrace, inside the Wanningsy. The *Chenyüan Chyliao*, based on the *Jyshia Kao*, says that this centre terrace was equidistant from east, west, north and south. If this was true, the east wall should have been farther east. Bretschneider was aware of traces of a very old rampart about 3 *li* outside the east wall, between Tungpienmen and Chihuamen (see map). But he could not determine what it was, since these ramparts appeared much lower and older than those on the north side. Also Chinese works never mention these old traces in this connection.

On the north side, however, the old Mongol ramparts can still be seen. In 1917, while teaching at Tsinghua University, I climbed the Mongol walls, 5 *li* outside the north wall, which is seldom done, either by Chinese residents or foreign tourists. The whole area outside Tehshengmen is not even what we mean by a suburban area; it is completely rural in aspect, with farmsteads and duck ponds. There was a large body of water just outside the northwestern corner, which accounts for the considerable bend of the city wall at this place, and incidentally also for the greater length of the north wall as compared with the south wall.

Among all writers that I know, Chinese or foreign, Bretschneider alone gave a detailed description of these Mongol ruins. Trained as a scientist,[39] he gave

an account which is worth reproducing: [40] " In fact, if one leaves from one of
the northern gates of present Peking, one finds, 5 *li* to the north, an ancient wall,
well preserved, which one can follow for a distance of more than 7 English miles
and which connects up with the northwestern and northeastern corners of the
Tartar city. I have examined this ancient wall (*tucheng*, or mud wall, in
Chinese), in its entire length. It is 20 to 30 feet high. It commences from the
moat situated at the northeast corner of Peking and goes north for a distance
of 5 *li;* then it runs west: at this corner, there appeared formerly to have been
a great tower, if one may judge by the plateau and circular form found at this
place. When the wall, continuing westwards, reaches the line forming a con-
tinuation of the west wall of Peking, it turns south. At this corner, there was
another tower. The ancient wall disappeared into a reservoir, situated near the
northwest corner of Peking. At a distance of about 150 paces, it is flanked on
the inside by regular projections (bastions) similar to those which could be seen
on the present Peking walls. Many paths and cart roads, leading towards or
away from the city, cross the ancient wall; but a close examination shows that,
at first, only four gates pierced this wall: two on the north, on a direct line

207

from the Antingmen and the Tehshengmen; one on the east, and one (or perhaps two) on the west. For at these points, the east wall is cut by large passages. The two openings on the north are known popularly as the Tungshiaokuan and Shishiaokuan (little passes, east and west). At Shishiaokuan, which is situated directly opposite the Tehshengmen and crossed by the route to Kalgan and Kiakhta, one can see a mud tower on the crest of the wall. It is hollow inside, but there is no door to it.[41] The western wall has a gate, about one English mile from the northwest corner of present Peking. Through this gate passes the main route between the Tehshengmen and the Summer Palace.[42] Outside the gate, one finds a circular wall as high as the rampart of the old city, situated against it, but not touching it. This wall encloses a space with an area of several hundred square yards, where there is a temple apparently of a more recent origin. The circular wall was perhaps formerly part of a fort. Not far from the northwest corner of this ancient rampart (that is to say, on the south of the corner), one sees on the top a pavilion with a yellow roof, known to the people by the name of Huangting (Imperial Tower). In this pavilion is a great marble tablet, carrying on one side the inscription in four big characters, *Chi Men Yen Shu*, and on the other side, a verse written by Emperor Chienlung of the last century, concerning the *Chi Men Yen Shu* which was the name of a park situated exactly on this spot...''

Bretschneider goes on to say that he could not make up his mind whether this was the ancient city of Chi, or the Mongol City, but decided in favour of the latter. His doubt was due to the fact that the Ming writers never referred to this place as " The Mongol City " but by the classic name of Chi. It seems clear to me from the records about the Copper Horse Gate that Chi was situated here from the first millennium B. C. to a few centuries A. D., and that its city limits could well have been a part of the northwest corner of the present city. It should occasion no surprise to a Chinese that the Ming poets always referred to it as Chi, because in poetry and *belles lettres* the classic ancient names are always preferred. Do not use an obvious reference, when an obscure one is available. It sounds more elegant!

Marco Polo gave the city limits of Peking as 24 miles around, in other words about 6 miles on each side. This would make it approximately 70 *li* in circumference. Western scholars like Siren and Bretschneider, as well as Chinese records, show this estimate to be excessive. Sirén says that it " could hardly have been over 50 *li*.[43] Bretschneider, after very careful consideration, came to the conclusion: " If my suppositions are exact, the limits of Khanbaligh should have been about 50 ordinary *li* around (a little less than 13 *li* from north to south and 11.64 from east to west)." Both the *Chuokenglu* and the *Peiping Tuching Chyshu* estimated the Yüan city to be 60 *li*. In view of modern measurements and the definite information which we have, I must accept Bretschneider's conclusions.

The Mongol city was certainly larger than the present city, which is about 42 *li* around. There is no doubt that the Mings lopped 5 *li* off the north end of the Mongol city, leaving out not only the two gates on the north Mongol city wall, but also one on the east wall and one on the west wall, both near the north corners. This explains why today the two gates on the east wall and the west wall show a certain imbalance; for instance the Shichymen is much closer to the northwest corner than it would be normally. Several Chinese historical sources say that this reduction took place at the very beginning of the Ming régime when Shü Ta was directing the construction of the new Ming city.

Some ambiguity exists as to the southern limits of the Mongol city. Sirén accepts Bretschneider's conclusion that the Mings had pushed the southern ramparts farther out and that the Mongol city line was probably 1 ½ *li* inside the present Chienmen. This ambiguity was recognized by the editors of *Jyshia Kao* who summed up the situation as follows (vol. 38, p. 2):

" The Yüan capital was 60 *li*. At the beginning of Ming, Shü Ta shortened its northern half on the east and west when he was planning Peiping.[44] Hence one sees a succession of mud elevations at Tuchengkuan outside Tehshengmen. These are all remains of the Yüan north city wall. As to its south side, history does not mention any changes having been made. But both *Yüan Tungyi Chy* and the *Shitsin Chy* [45] stated that when the officers of the Mongol capital were setting out the line for the city, they came to the pagodas of the two priests Haiyun and Ko-an at Chingshousy. The order was given to build the wall 30 paces around them. Now the Shuangtasy (Two Pagoda Temple), which is the former Chingshousy, still stands on the north of West Changan Street, almost two *li* away to the north from the Shüanwumen. Following this evidence, it seems to us that the present south wall does not quite fall in line with the ancient site of Mongol times. For at the beginning of the Ming Dynasty, the Mongol city was shortened on the north side and extended a little on the south."

Bretschneider showed some hesitation in reaching his conclusion. He mentions the Two Pagoda Temple case, which led him to believe that the Mongol South Wall logically followed that line, but on the other hand, the distance given in other sources between the palaces and the south central gate (Lichengmen) would place it exactly where the Chienmen today stands. Finally, he was struck by a note in *Chunming Mengyu Lu* (a work concerning various temples and palaces) stating that the Observatory was in the city's northeast corner, which is about 1 ½ *li* from the present south wall, and decided in favour of a line receding northwards from the present south wall. He said that in drawing his map he had to make a decision; and that shows his uncertainty.

During the twelfth century when the South Sung kingdom was a tributary power to the Chin Kingdom, many important records were made of trips made to the Chin capital by emissaries of the South Sung Dynasty. The editors of the *Jyshia Chiuwen Kao* (vol. 37, p. 25) enumerate six of these records of missions, all of the South Sung Dynasty, of which those by Shü Kangtsung, Fan Chengta and Chou Hui are the most important. In addition, they list twenty records of missions to Chin (negotiations for peace, congratulations on birthdays, and so on) which had mostly disappeared and existed in quotes and references only, as well as ten others which had been collected in a compilation on peace negotiations with the Chin rulers but were not certainly complete, and eleven others known by name only. Fan Chengta (1126-1193) was a great traveller, and left records of his travels in north, south and west China. Five or six of such records (usually rather thin volumes, equivalent of one to three chapters) are still available today. Among these the following are easily accessible in the *Tsungshu Chicheng* (" collection of collections ", published by the Commercial Press, Shanghai): Fan Chengta, *Lanpilu*; Lu Chen, *Chengshaolu*, and Lou Yu, *Peishing Jychi* (Diary of a Northern Journey).

It is generally agreed that the north wall of Peking both in Liao and Chin times extended to a line near the south wall of the present city, a little north of Poyunkuan, where the old Liao ramparts are. On the south the Chin capital extended to the neighbourhood of Fengtai in the southern suburbs, where another longer section of the old ramparts, over two miles long, can still be seen. Bretschneider and the *Jyshia Kao* are of the opinion that the Chin Forbidden City was *outside* the southwest corner of the Outer City. All writers, including Favier and Sirén, concede that the south wall of the Chin city must have been at least 2 ½ *li* outside the present south wall of the Outer City. Chü Shüanying states his view as follows: " In general, the Chin City includes the *Tiaoyutai* [Fishing Terrace, west of Poyunkuan], which was the Tungloyuan of the Chins on the northwest, the present Shiyuan [the Three Seas area], which was the Wanankung of the Chins on the northeast, and the modern Fengtai on the southwest. The central south gate of the Chin city was called Fengyi, from which Fengtai derives its name. Its southeastern corner reaches the Nanyuan of today " (*Peiching Chienchy Tankwei*, p. 1). This would give the Chin capital a lopsided appearance, with its northwest corner much shorter than its northeast corner.

The Chinese records suggest that the Chin capital was quite square. Three records show that it had twelve gates, three on each side, names them and gives the directions they faced. One record, the official *Chin History*, named thirteen, adding the Kwangtai Gate. However, the *Shitsinchy* (Ancient District History of Peking) after describing the new city built in 1151 and the twelve gates, says " Two gates were *changed*, called Tsingyi and Kwangtai," (*Jyshia Kao*, vol. 37, page 14). It seems that this refers to the old Liao gates which had been altered or renamed, as the north wall remained practically the same. It is also possible that a new gate on the north was opened nearer the present Chienmen side, which for convenience led straight northwards to the summer palaces of the Three Seas area.

The *Jyshia Kao* quotes Shü Kangtsung's record of his mission to the Chins in the early part of the twelfth century as saying that " The district city of Yenshan has a circumference of 27 *li*, with gate towers forty feet high. There are 910 towers, 3 successive moats and 8 gates." The editors comment: " This refers to the old city of Yenching. In 1151, according to Tsai Kwei's inscription at Tachüehsy, written in the Chin period, 3 *li* was added, making a total of

30 *li*. These all refer to the capital city. As to the 75 *li* given in the *Tachinkuo chy* (Record of the Great Chin Kingdom), it refers to the outer defences, just as we have the outer city today " (vol. 37, p. 16).

The evidence is quite clear that the ancient Chin city was cross-shaped at first, or had a separate fort on each side, before the Prince of Hailing expanded it. The *Jyshia* of Chu Yichun quotes *Chinkuo Nanchien lu* (Story of the Southward Moving of Capital of the Chin Kingdom) as saying: " Nikan, Prince Chungshien (later second king of Chin) had the idea of making Yen his capital. He kept the Liao imperial palaces and structures in the Inner City, but built on the outside four cities,[46] each city being 3 *li*. Each had a front and a back gate, and was provided with towers, movable scaffolds (for archers) and moats, like a frontier city. In each of them were stored grain, shields and weapons. Each was connected with the inner city by a *futao*.[47] Usheh, Prince of Chen, and General Han Changloso smiled at his over-caution, and Prince Chungshien replied, 'In a hundred years, ti will be seen that my view is well taken'. When Prince Hailing (A.D. 1149-1160) made Peking his capital and having built his palaces, desired to tear down these (fortified) cities, Tsai Tienchi said, 'Chung-shien was an important founder of the dynasty. He must have had his reasons for building them'. The plan was then dropped."

Bretschneider made a personal survey of the old ramparts some 8 *li* southwest of the southwestern corner of the Outer City. (I translate here from the French [48] (pp. 24-5) as I do not have the 1876 English translation published in Shanghai.)

"The rampart of an old city is found at about 8 *li* southwest of the Changyi-men (Kwangningmen), and about the same distance from the Yu-anmen, which is the western gate on the south wall of the Chinese city. Leaving this about 2 *li* to the south, one comes upon a little stream running from west to east, across the swampy area and some ponds. I followed upstream along its course. Going up several *li* on its north bank, one comes upon an ancient rampart, 20 to 30 feet high, which runs parallel to the river. For more than 7 *li*, one can follow this rampart, which in general is well preserved. At a hamlet, called Ofangying (Goose Camp), the rampart makes a bend towards the north. Evidently here was the southwest corner of the old city. Before coming to the stone-paved road, the wall disappeared. This corner is very picturesque; and at this point, the wall is covered with superb white pines (*pinus Bungeana*) and tall junipers. A hundred paces to the west is a cemetery called the *Hei Kung-fenti* (Black Public Cemetery), surrounded by a wall which encloses splendid thickets of white pines and junipers. About 2 *li* to the southwest stood the village of Liuchun, which belongs to Fengtai. This last designation, dating from the times of the Chins, is now applied as a general name to a group of villages famous for their flowers. According to the popular tradition, the rampart in question was always a part of the Chin capital; and this tradition is not in conflict with the documents furnished by Chinese writers on the ancient Chungtu. There exist also traces of an old city wall a few hundred paces north of the Poyunkuan monastery. There lies probably what was the north wall of the Chin city."

Several erroneous ideas are due to a map drawn by Father Alphonse Favier. He shows the extension of the Chin capital to be exactly south of the present Inner City and practically coextensive with the present Outer City. This error requires consideration.

That the Chin built upon the Liao city is known to all scholars. That the Liao, Chin and earlier Tang city lay to the southwest of the Inner City is supported by overwhelming evidence. It lay for the most part *outside* the present Outer City, and in part covered a section of its western half. The outer contour of the expanded Chin city is not entirely clear, especially if it was irregular. It may have projected into the Three Seas area on the northeast, which would have brought it right into the middle of the Forbidden City. But nowhere was there any historical reference or material evidence to suggest the Chin city had merely extended eastward towards the present Outer City.

The most important evidence is the Tutimiao (Temple of the Earth God) of the metropolis, which enables us to locate the *north gate* of the Chin capital. The *Tuching Chyshu* records that this temple was on the west of Tungyuanmen Street in the ancient Chin city. We can therefore indicate with a fair degree of certainty where the north gate, the Tungyuanmen of the Chin capital, stood. The Tutimiao is now situated in Tutimiao Alley, to the southwest of the Shüanwumen.

The *southeast border* is pretty well indicated by a stone inscription. The Minchung-sy of Tang times, now called the Fayuansy, was built in A. D. 645 by the Tang Emperor Taitsung in memory of the war dead in his Korean campaign. In this temple is an old inscription commemorating the re-sealing of a Buddhist relic (*shehli*) dated A. D. 892, which says, " Inside the great Yen city, at its southeastern corner, is the Minchungsy, looking out on a main street." This temple is now inside the Outer City, about midway between its north and south wall, quite far south of the Liulichang area, and a little to the west of a line directly south from Shüanwumen.

The *eastern* limit of the ancient city can be deduced from two pieces of evidence: (a) The present Liulichang, famous for secondhand book stalls and antiques (genuine and forged), is described in a tomb inscription discovered in the eighteenth century ("recently" according to the editors of the *Jyshia Kao*), which says that the tomb was in the "Haiwang Village, *outside* the East Gate of Yenching." The Liulichang is on the southwest of Chienmen, outside the central gate of the Inner City. (b) At the Black Pottery Kiln (Heiyaochang), there is a stone monument commemorating Monk Huichy, dating back to the Shouchang reign (really Shoulung, *lung* being a taboo character [49]) (A. D. 1092-1100), describing the place as "*outside* the East City." This is just west of the temple of Agriculture. These two records settle the eastern border of the Tang and Liao city pretty definitely.

Continuing west from the Tutimiao, mentioned above, there are two famous temples known in the times of both Chin and Liao. First, there is the Tienningsy (the Tienwangsy of the Chin period), which is just outside and a little to the north of the west gate of the Outer City. The *Yuan Tungyi Chy* describes it as situated inside the Chin capital and under the jurisdiction of the Yenchingfang, which is a police precinct. Farther out, to the northwest of this temple is Poyunkuan, where lived Chiu Chuchi, the famous Taoist priest who met Jenghiz Khan. It is near the modern race-course, almost on a line west of the Shipienmen. On the southwest of the Poyukuan was the Kwangfosy, which was the Fengfosy of the Chins. A stone inscription about Tsao Chien, dated to the reign of Taiho, A. D. 1201-1208, says that it was "*inside* the city." We are now already approaching the fragment of a rampart which the local people call the old city of Queen Shiao of Liao.

The editors of the *Jyshia Kao* conclude: "We see from the above that the old capital of Liao and Chin must have been toward the western part of the present Outer City, extending beyond into its suburbs. Its northeastern corner must have been approximately contiguous with the southwestern corner of the present [inner] City. Furthermore, the *Chungtang Shychi* of Wang Hui of the Mongol Dynasty says that the author left for Kaiping on March 5, in the first year of Chungtung, A. D. 1260. He stayed the first night in the northern suburb near the Tungyuan gate [Chin gate]. At noon on the sixth, he stopped for rest at Haitien, '20 *li* from Yen city'. This is the Haitien of today, written with a different character. Calculating the distance in mileage, according to Wang Hui's evidence, it is not difficult to form a rough idea of the location of the outer works of 75 *li* of the Chin period.

"Again, the *Peiching chy* says that in the fourth year of Chy-yuan [Kublai Khan] formerly established his throne 3 *li* northeast of [Chin] Chungtu. Now the Chungtu was originally the old city of Tang, expanded by Liao and Chin only by several *li*; see Tsai Chüeh's inscription at the Tachüehsy. The Minchungsy *remained always in the southeastern corner* [italics mine] of the [Chin] city" (vol. 38, p. 4).

Chu Yichun, author of *Jyshia* comments, "The Hungyehsy of the Sui and the Tang period was inside the capital. The Minchungsy of Yuchow of Tang was in the eastern part of the city. The Yenching of the Liao period remained on the same site." Then he adduced a new piece of evidence, showing that the present Shi-anmen inside the Inner City, directly west of the long Jade Rainbow Bridge separating the Middle Sea from the North Sea, was "5 *li* *northeast* of the ancient Tang Yuchow." He says:

Dresses of military officiers

" In the year 1681, a palace officer, while breaking the ground for a residence, discovered inadvertently an ancient tomb. There were an earthen stove, an earthen jar, and two tombstones, each one foot two inches wide. One of them says it was the tomb of a Madame Pien. Around these words was a circle of figures with animal heads and human bodies, representing the twelve animals of the birth cycle. The other tablet read, 'This is the epitaph of the Madame Pien of Puyang of the Great Tang Dynasty. In the 5th year of Tsengyuan (A. D. 799), on the *Kweimao* day of the seventh month, Madame died in the Chipei precinct of Chi Country of the Yuchow district. The same year she was temporarily buried on the plains of Lishien village, *5 li northeast of the Yuchow capital*'."

Chü Shüanying, author of *Peiching Chienchy Tankwei*, quotes the *Tienchy Ouwen* as saying that 2 *li* west of the Palichuang (" Eight-*li* Village ") is the river Shyliho (" Ten-*li*-River ") otherwise called " Queen Shiao's Canal." On its eastern bank is clearly discernible a mud rampart, called locally " Queen Shiao's City." This is the Queen Shiao of the Liao period. He adduced another piece of evidence from the *Liao History*, which speaks of the *Yenchiaolou* (" Yen Corner Tower ") at its northeastern corner. Now, just inside the Kwangningmen (West Gate of Outer City) is an alley named Yenchiao (Yen Corner) Hutung.

Bretschneider, who examined all the evidence very closely at first hand, concludes (p. 24): " The preceding documents provided by Chinese authors and based on ancient monuments, leave no doubt about the position of ancient Peking, since the seventh century, and one can assume that the *Tang* period city and the capitals of the *Liao* and *Chin* were situated approximately in the same place; that is to say, a little to the southwest of the present Tartar City and that *their eastern wall was in the western part of the Chinese city* " [italics mine]. Note that Bretschneider accepts the traditional view concerning the location of the Chin capital.

I have been at some length to correct the erroneous notion now current in English books that the Chin capital was *directly south* of the Inner City, where

the present Outer City lies. This error comes from Favier in his *Péking, Histoire et Description*. Favier gave the first map (p. 18) of the Chin capital as a new city built on the east of the old Liao capital adjoining it, and of approximately the same size as the Liao city; on the east side the new capital falls in line with the present east wall of the Outer City, and on the west side, a little short of the present west wall. The two standard works in English on Peking, Juliet Bredon's *Peking* (1924) and L. C. Arlington and Wm. Lewisohn's *In Search of Old Peking* (1935), and the guide book in French, *Pékin*, by Maurice Fabre (1937), all reproduce these elaborate maps showing the relative sites of the cities in the various periods: [50] the ancient Chi city, and the cities of Tang, Liao, Chin and Yüan and the present city. The most baseless assumption is the drawing of a Chin Forbidden City where the Temple of Heaven now stands. Osvald Sirén confines himself to reproducing separate maps in his authoritative *Walls and Gates of Peking* (1924), saying (p. 17) that the maps are taken from the *Guide Madrolle* and *Le Bulletin Catholique de Péking* 1914; thus the sources still go back to Favier.[51]

In general, Favier took the common term during the Mongol period denoting the old city as "south city" to mean that it was exactly south and was able to quote one source which used this term. He also tried to account for the perimeter of the Chin capital by including in it the Liao capital, regarding them as two cities forming a rectangular shape, twice as long east-west as north-south. From this premise, he points out that the Chins never destroyed the old Liao city but expanded it, which is quite true. When he says, " as the historic documents show us, [they] *built on its east side* [italics mine] a new city, which, with the old one, formed the new capital of Chin and was called Chungtu," the statement is incorrect. The historic documents never record that the Chins built a new city on its east side, but rather that they built four new forts clearly meaning *on all sides*, each 3 *li* in circumference, connected by tunnels with the main city.

Favier points out that the Chins had summer palaces where the present Three

Seas are, which is quite correct. He says that the *Peiping Tuching Chyshu* affirms that the Mongol capital was constructed 3 *li* north of the city of Chin. " These designations would be short of being exact if the location of the Chin city had been the same as that of the Liao capital " (p. 19). I must point out that the southwest-northeast relative position is given repeatedly in many sources and cannot be ignored in favour of one single record that says " north " instead of " northeast," and that the term " south city " was used popularly, as no one would take the trouble to be always geographically exact in common talk. This cannot be adduced as evidence. Favier further states that " Marco Polo says that Kambalick was contiguous to the old city of Chin, and that only a river separated them. The two cities had then at least about the same length on its banks." This is entirely unwarranted. Two cities could meet in a southwest-northeast relative position and still be separated only by a river. Favier admits that the old temples furnishing the evidence are all in the southwest corner, but " one understands that the new city could not have monuments." This seems a lame excuse, for the Chin capital lasted a hundred years. He says that the Chins built inside the new city a new imperial residence. This is correct, but the location of the imperial residence depends entirely on where you interpret the new city to be. Favier thinks that the new city had a circumference of 30 *li* and this, with the Liao city of 36 *li*, would make a total of 66 *li*. This approaches the historical record of a perimeter of 75 *li*.

The mass of evidence is all against Favier. There is not one specific piece of evidence to make one think that his conclusions were correct, although there is also no question but that the city's eastern suburbs, now corresponding to the Outer City, were densely populated, both in Chin and in Marco Polo's times.

NOTES

¹ See fuller discussion of the city's dimensions in Appendix I.

² *The Book of Ser Marco Polo* edited by Henry Yule, notes by Henri Cordier, Vol. I, p. 365-6. Marco Polo's description of the hill places it at "the north of the Palace" which is where Coal Hill stands. Some authorities think that he was describing the Chiunghua Isle in the North Lake. Against this opinion is the fact that Marco Polo would have mentioned it as an island on a lake if this was what he meant. The local name, Coal Hill, comes from the idea that originally it contained coal for the city in case of a siege. The literary name is Chingshan, or Prospect Hill. See Arlington & Lewisohn, *In Search of Old Peking*, p. 125, as well as notes by Yule.

³ The square brackets indicate Ramusio's text.

⁴ See Bland and Backhouse, *Annals and Memoirs of the Court of Peking*, 1914.

⁵ The Yellow Emperor was a semi-mythical figure, a founder of Chinese civilization, from whom all Chinese claim their descent. In any case, he was associated with the region of Peking in his legendary battles southwest of the city. It was here too, at Choukoutien, 30 miles southwest of Peking, that the "Peking man", the pleistocene *sinanthropus pekinensis*, was found in 1927.

⁶ It is always a curious fact that Chinese art flourished whenever she was politically at her lowest ebb. Whenever freedom of thought was curtailed, art at least offered a form of self-expression. Art and scholarship were substitutes for an active life and complete isolation from politics made absolute devotion to the creative arts possible. This was true of some of the great painters during periods of the Chin, Mongol and Manchu conquests.

⁷ Chu was a great poet and indefatigable scholar; he was one of the editors of the official *Ming History*, had access to the emperor's private library inside the palace, and enjoyed the favour of Emperor Kangshi, who treated him almost as a personal friend. He travelled extensively, but while in Peking lived in the northwestern corner of the Outer City, at the site which he regarded as the centre of the Chin capital. The emperor also gave him a house near the Drum Tower. He made it his business to record every stone and brick of the ancient sites of Peking, and had enormous patience for detail. His life was made the more touching and memorable for his affair with his wife's sister, who died for love. In *Jyshia*, he collated and put together every possible reference to sites and streets and temples and palaces of Peking in various histories and literary works, so that most of the sources are found arranged in this book.

⁸ The *Jyshia* compiled in 1688 is in 42 "volumes", and the revised *Jyshia Kao* of 1744 expanded it to 160 volumes (In length one "volume" is the equivalent of about one chapter in western books.) This material was so extensive that Wu Changyuan in about 1770 made a digest of it, reducing it to a kind of pocket historical guide to Peking, called *Chenyuan Shyliao*. The full name of the book is *Jyshia Chiuwen*, and the revised version *Jyshia Chiuwen Kao* (*Researches on Jyshia Chiuwen*).

⁹ Father Hyacinthe Bitchurin's (a Russian doctor, also written Bichurin) *Description of Peking*, 1829, was the first study, based on translations from the *Shenyuan Shyliao* (see above footnote) and for a long time this work in Russian was the only material available. In the eighteen-seventies, Dr. Emil Bretschneider made the best and clearest presentation of the material; he availed himself of the Chinese material, chiefly drawing on the *Jyshia*, and also made special journeys to verify the ruins of the Mongol and Chin city walls. He is extremely accurate and always gives his sources. His monograph "*Recherches Archéologiques et Historiques sur Pekin* (French translation, 1879) is no more than 97 pages, plus some 30 pages of notes but in addition to contributing some first-hand verification, remains the clearest summary.

[10] *Jyshia*, vol. 38, pp. 11-12.

[11] For detailed data, see Appendix III.

[12] *Jyshia*, vol. 29, p. 13.

[13] Marco Polo, vol. I, p. 356.

[14] Marco Pool, pp. 381-84.

[15] See *Lady Wu*, by Lin Yutang, Heinemann, 1957.

[16] A few terms denoting the different types of structure should be explained. In this book the term Tai Ho Tien, for instance, is spelled as Taihotien, and Ha Ta Men is spelled as Hatamen, because the Chinese think of Hatamen and Taihotien as unitary concepts (just as Shanghai is not spelt Shang Hai). Sometimes an English word is added; they may speak of the Hatamen Gate, even though *men* means a gate. It is always better to use these names as they are pronounced in Chinese and by Chinese. Thus Taishan is to the Chinese a complete concept, and the spelling is preferable to an English expression like the Tai Mountain. These words, *men, tien*, etc., therefore frequently appear as the last syllable of names for places or structures.

kung		palace; palace compounds, as in *Kunningkung*.
tien	=	sacred hall in palace or temple, as in *Taihotien*.
tang	=	any hall; church, as in *Nantang* and *Peitang* (Catholic in Peking).
ching	=	capital, conventionally written *king*, as in *Nanking*, *Peking*.
shan	=	hill or mountain, as in *Taishan*, *Wanshoushan*.
ho	=	river, or stream, as in *Huangho* (Yellow River), *Sangkanho*.
hu	=	lake, as in *Kungminghu*.
hai	=	strictly " sea ", but used to denote the three imperial lakes, the *Nanhai*, *Chunghai* and *Peihai* (south, middle and north). In Mongol times this area was known simply as *Haitse*.
men	=	gate, door, as in *Hatamen* Gate. Pronounced " *mun* ".
sy	=	a Buddhist temple, as in *Lungfosy*, *Piyunsy*.
kuan	=	a Taoist temple, as in *Poyunkuan*.
miao	=	a Confucian or Buddhist temple; an ancestral temple is always a *miao*, never a *sy*, as *Taimiao*.

The names of certain types of structures are more difficult to represent by simple English equivalents because the things themselves are different.

pailou	=	decorative archways.
huapiao	=	a single decorative column.
yuan	=	garden or park, as in *Yihoyuan*, *Yuanmingyuan*, the New and Old Summer Palaces.
lou	=	tower, or many-storied building, as in *Kulou*, Drum Tower.
ko	=	a highly situated building, or part of a tall building where distant views are visible. Really pronounced *ker*.
ting	=	a pavilion of various shapes, square, round, pentagonal, etc., sometimes with elaborate, even multiple roofs.
tai	=	open terrace.
shieh	=	hall with verandah overlooking the water, usually open on three sides.
shuan	=	a hall with one or more sides open; often used, however, for names of studios, as in Chienlung's *Kuyuehshuan*, famous for his porcelain.
lang	=	a covered corridor or gallery, open on one or both sides, leading from one court to another, provided with low balconied seats for idle strolls, and serving as covered passage in rain or intense sunshine.
chiao	=	bridge, as in *Lukouchiao*, the " Marco Polo Bridge ".

[17] *Peking*, p. 127.

[18] For photographs of this object and the jade jar, see Osvald Sirén, *The Imperial Palaces of Peking*, Plates 150 and 153.

[19] *Peking*, p. 103.

[20] Translated by Bland and Backhouse from Chinese documents in *Annals and Memoirs of the Court of Peking*. This is a fair example of the flavour of this book. Backhouse was a Chinese scholar and able to use Chinese sources fully. According to the best authorities, Tsungcheng hanged himself on the tree, not at the pavilion.

[21] *Peking*, pp. 145-6.

[22] At first *Shangti* (Supreme Ruler) and *Tien* (Heaven) were the names for God in two different ancient tribes. The sacrifice for *Tien* was called *chiao* (worship at the open " suburbs ") and the sacrifice for *Shangti* was called " *lei* ". Both were monotheistic. Later the two concepts merged.

[23] *Chinese Painting*, p. 175.

[24] William Rockhill Nelson Museum, Kansas.

[25] *Round About My Peking Garden*, p. 203.

[26] Le Coq, *Buried Treasures of Chinese Turkestan*, Allen & Unwin, 1928.

[27] Marco Polo, chapters 48-50.

[28] James Cahill, *Chinese Painting*, pp. 89 ff.

[29] S. Mizuno and T. Nagahiro, *Yun-kang*, 15 vols., Japan, 1950 onwards.

[30] Chiang Yee, *Chinese Calligraphy*, London, 1938.

[31] Chiang Yee, *Chinese Calligraphy*, p. 12.

[32] Lin Yutang, *The Gay Genius*, London and New York, 1947.

[33] O. Sirén, *Chinese Painting: Leading Masters and Principles*, London, 1958.

[34] Sir Harry Garner, *Transactions of the Oriental Ceramic Society*, 1959-60, p. 23.

[35] John Alexander Pope, *Chinese Porcelain from the Ardebil Shrine*, U.S.A., 1956.

[36] Lady David, *Illustrated Catalogue of Ching Enamelled Wares in the Percival David Collection*, 1958, pp. x-xiii.

[37] S. Howard Hansford in *The Arts of the Ming Dynasty*, Oriental Ceramic Society, 1958.

[38] Sir Harry Garner in *The Arts of the Ming Dynasty*, Oriental Ceramic Society, 1958.

[39] Dr. Emil Bretschneider was a botanist and author of *Botanicon Sinicum: Notes on Chinese Botany from Native and Western Sources*, 3 vols., Trübner, London, 1882, and *Mediaeval Researches from East Asiatic Sources*, 2 vols., Trübner, London, 1888. See *Science & Civilisation in China*, Joseph Needham, Cambridge, 1954, vol. 1, p. 269.

[40] *Recherches Sur Pekin*, p. 32-35. (The translation from the French is mine. L. Y.)

[41] This is of course a signal tower, using bonfires as signals, as are found on the Great Wall. This would be the first of the signal towers to the northward, visible from the Bell Tower in the city.

[42] This is the route by which the Empress Dowager fled from Peking in 1900.

[43] O. Sirén, *Walls and Gates of Peking*, p. 25.

[44] At the beginning of the Ming period, the capital was at Nanking, and Peking was known as Peiping.

[45] A district history compiled under the Mings.

[46] *Cheng* – actually forts.

[47] A covered passage or tunnel.

[48] Publications of *L'Ecole des Langues Orientales Vivantes*, 1879.

[49] It was the custom that characters serving as parts of emperors' names were taboo in that particular dynasty, and in all documents and books certain synonyms had to take their place.

[50] Arlington, p. 335; Bredon, p. 16; Fabre, p. 19.

[51] On the subject of the Chin capital, Sirén writes (p. 18): "The rather lengthy account of them in Shun T'ien fu chih is somewhat confused as no attempt has been made to reconcile divergent statements taken from different sources."

BIBLIOGRAPHICAL GUIDE

The following is a selective bibliography of Peking, its history, art and customs. It i intended as a concise guide to some of the more important sources of information and research, without attempting to be comprehensive. In the case of works in Chinese, mention is made only of the basic sources; in any case, the serious student will find references to over one thousand sources in the *Jyshia Kao*, mentioned below. The *Jyshia Kao* is the *vade-mecum* for all research material on Peking down to A. D. 1744, covering every brick and stone, every verse and documentation since the city's beginnings, and including works that are now lost.

For the city of Kublai Khan, Marco Polo gave extensive and often graphic descriptions: *Book of Ser Marco Polo*, edited by Henry Yule, 2 vols. Scribner's, 1903. Both Yule and Henri Cordier have done valuable research in identifying place names, incorporated in the footnotes.

A monumental and most impressive work on Peking is *Péking, Histoire et Description*, by Alphonse Favier (1837-1905), published by Lazaristes au Pétang (Peking), 1897; also in Lille, 1900. It contains 524 engravings of old drawings by Chinese artists. *Grandeur et Suprématie de Péking*, by Alphonse Hubrecht, Lazaristes, 1928, is actually a reissue of the work by Favier.

The work by Father Hyacinth Bitchurin (Nikita Yakovlevich, 1777-1853) is a translation (1829) into Russian of the Chinese *Chenyuan Shyliao* (1788), which latter is again a handy compilation of information in *Jyshia Kao*. Translated into French by Ferry de Pigny, this small work served as the sole source of information on the history of Peking in western languages, until Bretschneider came along.

Of all western researches on Peking, Bretschneider (Emil Vasilievitch, 1833-1901) was the one who was most conversant with the Chinese source materials. He was physician to the Russian Legation in Peking and a botanist. His *Recherches Archéologiques et historiques sur Pékin*

was first published by the American Presbyterian Mission, Shanghai, 1876, and translated into French by V. Collin de Plancy in 1879, published in *Publications de l'École des Langues Orientales Vivantes*, Paris.

Deservedly considered the best all-round book about Peking is *Peking*, by Juliet Bredon, 3rd revised edition, 1931. The niece of Sir Robert Hart, she wrote from her intimate knowledge, based on her personal roamings in the temples and hidden recesses of Peking and the Western Hills, in a charming, evocative and often beautiful style.

For factual, detailed information in a well arranged guide book, *In Search of Old Peking*, by L. C. Arlington and William Lewisohn, Henri Vetch, Peking, 1935, is unsurpassed. It contains many ground plans and reprints of some old wood blocks.

For books about historical events in Peking, the following by J. O. P. Bland and E. Backhouse can be highly recommended: *China under the Empress Dowager*, Heinemann, 1910 (centred upon the Boxer Uprising of 1900) reads like a detective novel, and *Annals and Memoirs of the Court of Peking*, Houghton, Mifflin, 1914, includes material from 16th to the 20th century, based on Chinese sources. *Court Life in China*, by Isaac Taylor Headland, Fleming H. Revell, 1909, gives interesting stories of the Empress Dowager and Emperor Kwangshü, covering the most important last decades of the Manchu Dynasty. *Indiscreet Letters from Peking*, by Putnam Weale (Bertram Lenox Simpson, 1877-1930) is a lively personal account of the sack of Peking in 1900. *Round about My Peking Garden*, by Mrs. Archibald Little, Fisher Unwin, 1905, covers the same period.

For pictorial representation of Peking, the most complete and authoritative are the two works by Osvald Sirén: *The Walls and Gates of Peking*, John Lane, 1924, with 109 photogravures and 50 drawings, and *The Imperial*

Palaces of Peking, in 3 vols., 1926. *Peking the Beautiful*, by Herbert White, Commercial Press, Shanghai, 1927, contains a large collection of tourist photographs. Rare and of special historical interest is the book of Japanese woodcuts, *Tangtu Mingsheng Tukwei*, 1804-5, which shows many interesting pictures of Peking court life and buildings at the beginning of the nineteenth century, and from which some line drawings in this book have been taken. Of special value is the *Wanshou Shengtien*, a scroll 166 feet long, giving a panorama of the city on the occasion of celebration of Emperor Kangshi's 6oth birthday in 1713, when the Manchu Dynasty was at its height of prosperity. This has been reproduced in woodcuts in several editions, including the Tienshihtsai lithograph edition of 1879, with a curious note in English: "This book was taken from the Book Temple of Yuan Ming Yuan (Old Summer Palace) the day the Palace was burnt, October, 1860." The end papers of this volume are taken from a section of this scroll.

A brief mention may be made of the principal works in Chinese. The one basic source is the *Jyshia Chiuwen Tsao* (abbreviated in the text as *Jyshia*) by Chu Yi-chun (1629-1709), a great scholar and friend of Emperor Kangshi. This is a collation of all known passages and references to the city in Chinese history and literature. It was regarded as so noteworthy that by imperial decree an editorial committee was set up by Chienlung to have the work expanded, resulting in the *Jyshia Chiuwen Kao* (*Jyshia Kao* for short in the text), in 1744, in 160 volumes. The most important are the city in general (vols. 37-8), in past epochs (vols. 29-36), streets and temples (vols. 43-61), the parks and suburbs (vols. 74-87).

A factual source is the *Shuntien Fuchy* (district history of Peking area), first edition 1593, revised 1886, the source of Osvald Sirén's studies.

Chenyuan Shyliao, by Wu Changyuan, 1788, is a handy condensation of the voluminous *Jyshia Kao*, in 16 chapters It contains some curious old maps. The *Chunming Mengyu Lu* (Traces of Spring Dreams) by Sun Cheng-tseh, 1592-1676, gives information on temples, buildings and court customs in the form of memoirs. The *Tiching Chingwu Liao*, by two great scholars Liu Tung and Yu Icheng, 1635, though of historical value, was so vitiated by the perversely obscure style of the Chung-Tan School that the great imperial editor Chi Shiaolan under Emperor Chienlung took the trouble to cut out many parts of it. In addition, a few contemporary or more recent works have been published in the Library of Peking Customs, *Peiching Fengtu Tsungshu*, including one small volume which records the pedlars' cries in the streets of Peking.

There are two good books on Peking festivals and customs. *The Moon Year* is by Juliet Bredon and Igor Mitrophanov, Kelly and Walsh, Shanghai, 1927. *Annual Customs and Festivals in Peking*, by Derk Bodde, Henri Vetch, Peking, 1936, is a translation of the Chinese *Peiching Shuishy Chy*, by Chang Chiang-tsai. *Sidelights on Peking Life*, by R. W. Swallow, 1927, is an interesting small volume, of a more elementary character.

ACKNOWLEDGMENTS

The Publishers wish to thank the following persons for their advice and help in the preparation of this volume:

Mr. J. G. Ayers, Victoria and Albert Museum, London;
Mr. James Cahill, Freer Gallery of Art, Washington;
Mr. Chen Yuan;
Mr. Leonard J. Grant, National Geographic Magazine, Washington;
Mr. Basil Gray, British Museum, London;
Mr. Li Tzu-yu, National Palace and Central Museums, Taiwan;
Miss M. Medley, Percival David Foundation of Chinese Art, London;
Mr. B. W. Robinson, Victoria & Albert Museum, London;
Mr. Laurence Sickman, William Rockhill Nelson Gallery of Art, Kansas;
Dr. Wang Shih-chieh, National Palace and Central Museums, Taiwan.

The photographs in this volume are reproduced by courtesy of the following authorities and photographers:

Ashmolean Museum
Ill. 71, 95, 105
British Museum – Edwin Smith
Ill. 86, 98, 100, 101, 113
W. H. Eagle
Ill. 31, 34, 35, 36, 83
Fitzwilliam Museum – Edwin Smith
Ill. 59, 93, 94, 99
Hsinhua News Agency
Ill. 81, 82
Ergy Landau
Ill. 1, 3, 6, 8, 10, 14, 15, 16, 17, 23, 25, 41
Magnum Photos
Ill. 4
Metropolitan Museum – H. C. Weng
Ill. 68, 91
Musée Guimet – Giraudon
Ill. 103, 115
Musée Guimet – J. A. Lavaud
Ill. 20
National Central Museum, Taiwan
Ill. 52, 54, 66, 96
National Geographic Society – W. Robert Moore
Ill. 5, 12, 22, 30
National Palace Museum, Taiwan
Ill. 37, 38, 39, 49, 51, 55, 60, 61, 62, 64, 65, 69, 73, 89, 92, 97, 112
National Palace Museum and Freer Gallery of Art
Ill. 44, 45, 47, 57, 78, 84
Percival David Foundation of Chinese Art
Ill. 53, 58, 80, 104, 107, 108, 109, 110, 116
E. Rosenberg and F. R. S. Yorke
Ill. 9, 11, 24, 27, 28, 29, 43
University Museum, Philadelphia – H. C. Weng
Ill. 67
Victoria & Albert Museum – Edwin Smith
Ill. 50, 72, 90, 102, 106, 111, 114, 117
Wango H. C. Weng Collection
Ill. 74, 87, 118, 119
William Rockhill Nelson Gallery of Art
Ill. 56, 63, 70, 75, 76, 77, 79, 85

INDEX

225